welcome complexity

Manifesto

Addressing Complexity

Weaving Together:
Reason and Strategy in
Human Affairs

First Edition

The Welcome Complexity logo and cover design were created by Ideoscripto on a complimentary basis. (ideoscripto.com) :

The publication of this book is sponsored by Fourth Revolution Publishing.

English translation of the First Public Edition in French – October 2017
ISBN 978-981-14-7772-0 (paperback
ISBN 978-981-14-7773-7 (Kindle e-book)
Print On Demand via LightningSource

Contents

By way of introduction

We, the founding members of *Welcome Complexity*, appeal to anyone wishing to regenerate[1] their life environment, to make it congenial for living and working together; to anyone who daily experience challenges that appear complex and feel frustrated at being unable to find satisfactory answers. We appeal to anyone who, nevertheless, are unbowed, aware that only trial and error, courageous perseverance and occasional hurt will uncover the ways of tomorrow and accept that there will be times of near overwhelming feelings of powerlessness and isolation.

We are "bad good boys." While showing willingness, we want to continue calling into question that which is not questioned (dogma, institutions, customs, laws, authority, ...). We *can* blaze trails

[1] The word *regenerate* may have surprised some readers. We use it to stress that there is no requirement to invent something new; the founding members are not yearning for *somewhere else* or *something more*. We mean simply that whatever fails to regenerate is bound to degenerate. The task is to re-constitute those things which are bound to degenerate in the absence of care and attention.

toward new horizons and widen the range of possibilities.

We enthusiastically envision encounters and the chance to evolve together. This manifesto is intended to prompt and bring about such encounters, inserting those interactions in a joint aspiration and a common calling, in an effervescent civic project. *Welcome Complexity* seeks to be the locus of this mediation, an *agora*, a network, a crossroads, a workshop, a watchtower, an institute.

We are convinced that we are many but dispersed. The density of our presence is increasing but has not yet reached the threshold of crystallization. There is as yet no place for us to meet, recognize each other, breathe afresh, confront each other, sharpen our awareness. We need to become conscious of that which unites us and identifies us. This is the shared aspiration that moves *Welcome Complexity*.

The aim of this manifesto is to assist you in discovering synergies between what moves you and what moves us: we do this by formulating how we perceive the context of our lives and the challenges to address. We must caution any reader seeking for concreteness and practicality: this text confines itself to the intent and vocation of *Welcome Complexity*. The treatment of *what* and *how* is limited to brief outlines in the Conclusion and the Appendices.

In addressing this intent, we were faced with a problem in authoring. Potentially, this manifesto would reach everyone, and in particular those who feel that our text challenges or attracts them. Given such a multiplicity and idiosyncrasy of experience, how could we engage each and every one in their current mental abode? Well, since the action invoked by our manifesto requires a continuous combination of concept, decision and action, we have chosen to articulate it into three parts, aligned with *three stages of a process common to every citizen.*

- The first part touches each of us as involved in the maintenance and transformation of our world: **an orientation to action and work;**
- The second part touches each of us as involved in co-ordination, as responsible for an organisation: **an orientation to** governance. We are all concerned, inasmuch as we are responsible at least for ourselves.[2]
- The third part touches each of us as we reflect upon our practice: **an orientation to concept-orientated thinking**. This concerns us all, inasmuch as we all think.[3]

---

[2] Note that leaders are not necessarily accountable, and those in position of responsibility do not necessarily have the experience of a leader. It remains that in our society the typical responsible agent is a senior manager, in a public, private or associative organisation.

[3] Note that a researcher is not necessarily a thinker who reflects on their practices, nor are all thinkers researchers. While in our society the typical thinker role is assumed by intellectuals, professors and researchers, our human dignity requires that we resist severing our action from our thinking, against a socio-cultural tendency to segment our society into researchers, leaders and operators.

No doubt each of us has preferences and propensities to act, govern or think. However, as human beings and citizens we are all:

- challenged to act, decide and think,
- involved simultaneously in action, responsibility and reflection,
- concerned in, and called to join, all three parts of this manifesto.

It follows that the later sections of the third part – on citizenship and anthropology – are fully relevant to those who would at first feel an affinity only with the first two parts.

There was another difficulty in addressing semantic choices. Regardless of temperament or age, each reader is variously familiar with the domain concerned or the semantics in use. Some, engaged in active civic experiments, are more fully acquainted with those concepts than more mature researchers who are well-known in their discipline[4]. During initial review of the manuscript, we have observed that the more conversant the reader is of issues of complexity, the more comfortable is the language of this manifesto. Conversely, readers less acquainted with complexity tend to feel that this language is *conceptual* and hard to grasp. This perception arises from the difficulty of connecting the words with living

---

[4] Many researchers think in their laboratories in terms of optimization and "simple" solutions, whereas young, committed persons understand critical deliberation where a collective, intelligible formulation is sought of a problem arising.

experience. The words in themselves are no more *conceptual* than those of other domains which are more familiar. Such a bias may cause a reader to miss the intent of a statement. Note that this experience in terms of challenge is precisely a measure of the distance between the reader and what we aim to convey. So, reader, if you find the concepts used here alien to you, this is an indication that you are directly concerned with the intent of *Welcome Complexity*.

A summary for citizens

As agent of the transformation

The challenge is to learn a daily praxis of acting and thinking in complexity, which sustains a regeneration of critical thought. Learning in this way of life and self-expression calls for a companionship: this is what Welcome Complexity offers to anyone who wishes it.

As aware of their responsibility

The increasing complexity of our environment is a major challenge for decision-makers: the questions which they face are more and more intense while at the same time traditional modes of thought and action prove increasingly inadequate to provide an intelligible grasp of the environment.

To track such evolution, decision-makers need simultaneously to adapt themselves and their organisations. The intent is to support their search for a vision and a practice inspired by the new modes of thinking and acting in complexity: to connect, to place in context, to act, while reflecting on one's experience. Welcome Complexity is dedicated to supporting their endeavours, to restore their ability to act, to anticipate upcoming crises and to act as catalysts of thoughtful adaptation for persons and organisations.

As reflecting on their practices

Welcome Complexity is a project of those citizens who strive to widen their outlook on the world, identifying opportunities for regenerating society, one step at a time, rather than treating complexity as a problem that could be isolated by a segmentation of phenomena. In such a project, the task is:

- To regenerate and enrich our ways of acting and thinking to adapt them to transformation challenges in our societies,
- To develop our capacity for critical attention to the context of our interventions,
- To build pathways suitable for our current problems,
- To develop a praxis aligned with such pathways,
- To join what has been disjoined, in art, philosophy and the sciences,
- To regenerate scientific knowledge,
- To shed light on living-together and acting-together in the city.

Overall, the intent is to sharpen the joy, the enthusiasm, of living together and acting together, by awakening in each of us the awareness of the tension associated with the contradictions of which we are made.

What is “Welcome Complexity”?

Welcome Complexity is a non-profit association created in 2017 and intended to promote the principles and practices of *thinking and acting in Complexity* within society at large.

The objects of this association are any action likely to:

- Contribute to learning modes of living and working together, with attention to complexity in a global, open context,
- Develop and catalyse the propagation and transmission of conditions favourable to learning, collective exploration and co-construction of vision and pathways,
- Provide operating environments rooted in, continuously regenerating with, pluri-disciplinary scientific research; this research

tending toward trans-disciplinarity within the paradigm of complexity, thereby fostering regenerated links between scientific knowledge and philosophical knowledge.

The choice of the name is aimed at transforming the emotion experienced by anyone perceiving complexity in the world: we must change our emotion of fear or anguish to one of enthusiasm for new openings, renewed creativity and possibilities to be discovered in a world where we acknowledge complexity. This world, when seen as complex, becomes a potential source of riches: we emerge from a general flattening, which reduces and simplifies, to a surging emphasis which yields understanding and enrichment, without claims to generalised valuation. The name is English in recognition of the worldwide intent and calling of the Association.

The logo was chosen to symbolise reunion, collective endeavour, acceptance, multiplicity, robustness in collective action, the wish to be part of a movement, a dynamics, and a collective that is both differentiated and united.

The project is that of a pragmatic tree, with leaves reaching on high, and with deep roots, commensurate with such height, delving in a substrate that is existential, anthropological, ethical and epistemic. *Welcome Complexity* asserts an allegiance to a systemic, constructivist, pragmatic and complex epistemology. To ensure a strong sense of direction, the Association relies on a benevolent and vigilant collective a "circle of wise men'[5]. Its first member is Edgar Morin, President of the *Association pour la pensée complexe*. He has "*from the outset underlined the potential relevance and the cultural and civic stakes of such an initiative: the progressive institutionalization of such a platform has become feasible*".

The founding members[6] of *Welcome Complexity* are all thoughtful practitioners with a concrete engagement in civic life. They make up a weave with criss-crossing threads each representing a distinct outlook on the challenges of working and living together: economy, psychology, socio-anthropology, major complex projects, engineering, organizational change, animation and coaching, ergonomics, body psychology.

The project of *Welcome Complexity* is supported by patrons and sponsors. As of publication date, we have not yet secured permission to mention their names. It has also, ever since its inception, been supported by an ever-growing network of persons who endeavour

5 This circle is still being established at the time of this publishing.

6 See Appendix 4. Currently, the membership of Welcome Complexity is an inadequate representation of women and of the world beyond Paris. We are all conscious of this and wish for our membership to be aligned with our objectives. Our current composition is in great part the pragmatic outcome of our history.

to develop thorough thinking in pluri-, inter- and trans-disciplinarity. These researchers cover the whole spectrum of thought about complexity (Appendix 4). Among other concerns, they address epistemology, philosophy, socio-anthropology, disciplines of design, cognitive science, systems modelling, systems science, Artificial Intelligence, psychology, psychoanalysis, etc.

Part 1:
Working and Linking

A challenge: Complexity[7] as Praxis[8]

The perceived challenge is to learn to work and live in complexity, with a global, open context.

The growing complexity of our environment presents a major challenge to citizens, whether leaders or followers: the fundamental questions facing each of us become more intense at the very time when traditional modes of thinking and acting progressively lose their power. *We realize that our lives henceforth must accommodate a paradigm of continuous transformation.*

The challenge of complexity primarily arises within our heads. Here is an *epistemological* challenge: complexity is not a feature of reality "*per se*", but of our relationship to reality.

Complexity is not just a challenge. It is an opportunity as well, if one chooses to accept it and face it. The evolution of our environment calls for

---

7 See Appendix 1 for a brief introduction to the concept of complexity

8 We mention praxis, rather than practice, because the practitioner is also involved. It is customary to make use of a triptych, knowledge, know-how, social skill. A praxis requires knowledge, which can be taught, and a know-how, which can be practiced; but it also involves social skills, a knowing to be with others, necessary for practical application: this has an ethical and moral dimension. Said triptych turns out to be inappropriate, on two counts: it dissociates three headings which form an inseparable whole; it assigns all three components to a common, reducing category of knowledge. The use of praxis underscores the necessity of conjunction and integration: action and knowledge are inseparable from the being capable of action and knowledge.

a new art of moving and continuously evolving according to context:

- We need to develop and integrate renewed ways of thinking and acting in complexity, at all scale levels (local, regional, national, international and global),
- We need to bring about *inter-culturality*, including inter-generationality, inter-disciplinarity and inter-nationality. *Inter-* is a key to thinking and acting in complexity: relationships among elements prevail over elements.

Older generations who, from their standpoint of experience, observe the shifting environment and the effervescence of youth, have the charge of passing on to new generations their knowledge of frameworks and processes that can support them in the conscious co-construction of a world capable of inspiring them.

Such frameworks and processes require sponsors, of watchers and of guides within multidisciplinary scientific research on complexity, as well as of epistemological and ethical roots for the proposed practices.

The members of *Welcome Complexity*: citizens who shoulder their responsibility and reflect on their practice

Given such challenges, some stubbornly deny the accumulation of impediments to our current modes of thinking and acting; others wish to revert to past practices. Yet we also note that some are becoming aware of opportunities in modes of thinking and acting in complexity, and that they form and increasingly dense subset of the population.

This subset of the population is made up of persons intent on the local development of adaptive responses to a complex environment. They realize that a local action cannot be designed according to some single criterion – certainly not simply on performance or on material wealth. Yet they also know that performance and wealth may be necessary means to our ends. They clearly know that no established powers can substitute for the endeavour of each individual to transform their modes of thinking and acting.

This subset of the population is not sufficiently dense at this point, and not well prepared to bring about a major shift. It represents an expectation, possibly a need for support to handle complex problems and emerge from their isolation. Our first perceived challenge is to serve such intensification.

Given this expectation, the present manifesto must reach:

- Those who feel responsible and their advisors, in any domain and at all levels of action;
- Those who consider themselves agents of transformation, all those who wish to bring their best contribution to *living and working together*, in any organisation (see Appendix 4), and who want to master and put to use certain modes of thinking and acting in complexity appropriate to co-constructing the world to which they aspire.
- Those who reflect, starting from any which initial discipline, with the aim of rendering authentic intelligibility of the universe without surrendering to thinking conventions, and who thereby have necessarily become multi-, inter- and trans-disciplinary.

Our project: to regenerate feedback loops between *how* and *why* by means of argument and critical inquiry

There are many who, each in their specific context, feel, experience, infuse meaning, construct a vision, then walk on local paths within a complex global world.

Welcome Complexity is not one more solution to a predefined problem; neither is it the statement of a problem for which a solution is sought. *The point is not to add one more element to the ubiquitous effervescence – whether individual or associative – which is emerging organically in the widening cracks opening in the classical modes of thought and action. Welcome Complexity* is offering a new scene: we propose to take position in the cracks of the effervescence itself, which is the precursor of an emerging paradigm, that is, a regeneration of the old modes of thought and action.

The project of *Welcome Complexity* is to *enhance and catalyse the propagation and transmission of conditions favourable to learning in any useful mode, to collective exploration of possible worlds, to rapid co-construction of the desired world and of pathways for its advent.*

This project is not *to intellectualize* the world, but to provide for operating conditions rooted in – and continuously regenerating with – scientific thought, reflection and research.

Culture: scouts and designers

Our culture engages scouts and journeymen in practices of complexity, who are also able to do concept work and to establish the roots of their practice in a renewed perspective on research. One main characteristic is the search for excellence in adapting to variable environments:

- on-going questioning of discrepancies between the proposed framework and our perception of reality: we seek to harmonize,
- a challenging of established situations when it seems required: we seek to transform,
- a life experience in many organisations where we have demonstrated our ability for research, for creation, for design, for entrepreneurship and for adopting new practices which better fit the context: we seek to explore and walk forward,
- an institutional posture of trusted advisor, of *King's jester*, even of *Jiminy cricket* or busybody: we seek to challenge and awaken,
- an ability to combine so-called *hard sciences* and human disciplines called *soft sciences*: we seek to refute such divisions and bring about a different, conjoining perspective,
- an ability to use a pragmatic approach by trial and error, exploring possibilities, building and refining responses until they are seen to be *satisfactory*: we grope and stumble around.

What moves us: regenerate together those arts which in the past were tested and renewed

As scouts and designers, we observe that there are ways of everyday life which are a lot more satisfying than what shows up daily in our organisations. Thinking and acting in complexity is an activity that emancipates and contributes to better living and working together.

We want to enable and catalyse the creation of fertile ground for present and future agents of transformation.

We want to be a space committed to the development of autonomy in persons – as they become actors in complexity – *in the context of their organisations*.

We want to be a space where research becomes the root of a common shared corpus of *Action in complexity*. The multiplicity of methods hinders their clarity and diffusion: yet they are only aspects – albeit singular – of the same corpus. The list is long, and a symptom of the fragmentation which obfuscates an underlying unity. In Appendix 2, we give both details and an insight into their common stem.

To advance these goals, we want to instigate and maintain a relationship with deciders and agents of transformation, concerning:

- The art and practice[9] of navigating a complex world;
- The art and practice of design and construction;
- The operating frameworks in which members grow, which enables them to face tomorrow's world;
- The continuous enhancement of these practices by the feedback of the learners' experience and by their rooting in renewed research
- More generally, any contribution to their ability to face the challenges of complexity[10]

---

9 Some readers may be surprised to find the word 'art' in a domain where they would know only practices. Here is a preliminary argument on this point. A common feature of art and practice is that they are sensitive to concrete reality and life experience and draw on resources and competencies. Both require skill in the driving of action and the construction of complex artefacts, which are contingent, doubt-ridden, ambiguous, uncertain, yet viable and efficient in their relevant context. The grasping of a situation by a human being – an organic whole – can only be a hybrid of many features: rational, sensible, ethical, aesthetic, ... It is possible to distinguish art from practice, but not to dissociate them. The notion of art emphasizes the uniqueness of a composition and displays a wide variety of personal or collective expression. The notion of practice emphasizes the will to act (the project) and those processes which organise action in its context.

10 Thinking in complexity, among other things, insists on conjoining indeterminacy and contingency, and at the same time the fact that not every event is equally possible. The sciences of complexity, particularly work on stochastic processes and critical self-organising states, are useful heuristics to understand such situations.

Our hope: create a living environment, sustaining exchanges to bring fresh air, resources and new insights

The most beautiful story that could one day be told of us is that we were acknowledged as a living place, whence no one ever returned without some new idea, some new contact, some new practice to apply at home; a place steeped in multi-, inter- and trans-disciplinary study.

We shall have made progress toward this goal when:

- This place becomes the rallying point for those who wish to develop renewed ways of thought and action, allowing anyone to step forward confidently and consciously, using robust tools, rooted in research and tested in practice,
- Life, thought and action in complexity shall be communicated as an art, experienced as a solidarity, thought of as a science, just as are the traditional practices of art and philosophy,
- The system which is currently considered as education and teaching shall have undergone transformation to the extent of offering a lifelong training in this art and this science, beginning from early childhood.

What we aim for: to develop the art of *rejoining*[11] and the art and science of *working and living together*

Enabling the Association's ecosystem to:

- Extract itself from the rut of blinkered thinking, unable to renew itself,
- Discover, experiment, acquire renewed ways of thinking and acting in complexity,
- Continue learning thought and action in complexity throughout life, from early childhood to death,
- Practice *katas*, or *scales*, of the art of navigating complexity,
- Adopt an adequate language,
- Investigate complex problems as they arise and formulate them in a way that opens up satisfactory pathways.

To achieve this, *Welcome Complexity* intends to:

- Establish a forum for fruitful encounters, weave relationships among people, connect cultures and facilitate dialog, between disciplines, between scale levels (local to international), between generations, etc.

---

11 We see rejoining as an interpersonal relationship, emphasizing the psychosocial need for information, a state of interconnectedness of persons, the insertion of a person in a system of connections with a rich load of meaning and finality.

- Stimulate resonances between diverse cultures and sensibilities (both antagonistic and complementary), catalyse the emergence and the growth of projects and initiatives, weave connections among them,
- Connect agents of transformation who share a concern for renewal into a community of *journeymen of complexity*,
- Establish a centre for the development of a science of action and design in complexity, more particularly a science of intelligent orchestration of individual intelligences at all scale levels.

Part 2:
Governing
and Self Governing

Introduction

This second part of the manifesto is intended:

- For those who feel a responsibility for elaborating a form of action which is adapted to the complex problems they experience, and especially for those whose practice has known strong resistance or even multiple failures, regardless of the means deployed, in the face of problems they strove to address: digital transformation, organization of production, interpersonal dialogue and cultural transformation, efficiency and resilience, ecosystemic integration, ...
- For those leaders who are ready to transform themselves, together with the transformations they are facilitating in an organization under their leadership.[12]

Our project is also, on our walk together, to examine and investigate such aspirations and constraints, which are all strongly context-dependent, aiming to clarify stakes and illuminate pathways. Among other things:

- Whenever formalism tends to obfuscate possible choices, give back dimension to anything that was 'flattened', under the label of 'unified' thought, to regenerate the gamut of possibilities,
- Restore mobility and openness, by discovering and experimenting with modes

---

12 See Appendix 2 for an indicative list of organization types.

of thought and action emphasizing *exploration of context and explicit statement of problems* (using investigation and conceptualization processes) rather than *means of resolving a poorly stated problem*,

- Carefully use a language that is not reified but always adequate to intent and context,
- Direct strategic projects while resisting the temptation of prematurely adopting a solution: instead, assert the need for consciously clarifying stakes and specifying the perceived problem,
- Become clearly aware that what we call *reality* is not reality but simply our viewpoint on reality, this viewpoint being subjective and conditioned by our previous experiences, by the context, by dominant ideology and by our intentions,
- Encounter, exchange and share with all those who are similarly concerned with renewal.

The current mutation of our environment offers a challenge of complexity where we must invent the pathways

1 An unprecedented mutation of increasing complexity

The 'digital revolution' is a deep mutation of modes of production and of modes of organization generally. It clearly affects the enterprise.

However, it cannot be fully understood without recognizing that it simultaneously affects all scale levels in our societies. While transforming organizations, it transforms the political, social and economic environment at the same time.

This transformation, among other things, involves a push for active participation by citizens, increasing ecological demands, new forms of participative governance, etc.

While current leaders are generally aware of impacts at several scale levels, they understand less well some deeper aspects which emerge from research. The digital transformation deals in *information and organization*, not, like previous ones, *in matter and energy*. The attendant knowledge and practices require a profound renewal of our modes of thought and action.

Yet the *matter-energy* layer remains necessary to the existence of the next layer. It imposes constraints, which we perceive as increasingly strong, on the traditional use we make of it. We begin to realize that the resources are ultimately limited and that we must alter our relationship to them.

Recognizing that the second layer is unique and distinct from the first in turn refreshes our viewpoint on matter-energy. This offers regenerated ways of conceiving our relationship to those resources, arising from a new, deep questioning:

- The question of the construction of artificial systems, no longer usable as individual *handy* tools, but instead forming a whole environment within which we live as a collective and with which we are in continuous interaction;

- The question of articulating matter-energy with information-organization[13]
- The question of positioning human activity in a world with limited resources.

2 A complexity which confronts each of us personally

Within organizations, the environment of leadership appears increasingly complex. Leaders are solicited in multiple and sometimes contradictory ways, at an accelerating rhythm. Everything seems uncertain and confusing.

How can we respond to this? Those who are engaged and feel responsible experience disorientation, a feeling of powerlessness and isolation, while others take refuge in fugue, self-protection or blocking.

As a consequence, the environment that such leaders fashion for their subordinates becomes alienating, exhausting, even degrading. These individual responses are strongly detrimental to the ability of organizations to adapt, at the time where they need it most. Such situations offer

---

13 Such formulation may seem abstract: but simply consider how information can be used to support dynamic, intelligent distribution of energy within a wide collective, which may drastically reduce the concrete consumption of physical resources

even more challenges for those leaders in charge of key points in the organization.

3 Old modes of thought and action are quickly superseded

There is a widespread feel that leaders offer a common, short-term discourse: this feel arises from certain projects, which lack vision because they are aimed at the short term or express a kind of thought seen as 'one-size-fits-all'. Leaders and advisors still rely widely on recipes from the past: they cannot think 'out of the box'. Proposals differ only in anecdotal ways; decisions quickly end in failure in the field, where real constraints would require a completely different approach.

4 Questioning is intensifying about induced major challenges

In this context of deep transformation, when yesterday's approaches have become inadequate to tomorrow's world, leaders are faced with more intense questions.

Without any claim to being exhaustive, we see five subsystems of questions appearing out of this turmoil –somewhat interdependent though largely autonomous; each represents a major challenge facing any organization leader:

- *Digital transformation*: which pathways to prepare in the face of current problems? What new business and economic models?
- *Organizing production*: What new modes of production should be designed? What

architectures of value and business, for what platforms?

- *Interpersonal dialogue* among different logics within organizations; what are the conditions which are favourable to co-conception, co-elaboration, co-development among persons holding for varying logics and viewpoints? What are possible co-constructions with the ecosystem of customers, suppliers, partners?
- *Organizational adaptability* to rapid changes in the context: what conditions are favourable to a global vision associated with local pragmatism? What conditions are favourable to allying performance, commitment and motivation? What conditions are favourable to relevant expression of each person's uniqueness within an organization? What conditions are favourable to cultural transition to such renewed modes of thought and action?
- *Fitting in one's environment*: What are the conditions which are favourable to an organization taking account of its ecological impact?

Thoroughgoing alternatives are appearing in response to these mutations

1 Within a fruitful effervescence: promising opportunities

Confronted with the challenge of this mutation, those who take their civic responsibility seriously have been active: society is moved into a growing effervescence in search of satisfactory solutions. Every dimension of the transition is now scrutinised with new thought and practices. Some of these currents have been developing discreetly over decades: renewal of practices, of governance, of socio-political and economic approaches; new trends in research[14].

2 A need for discernment, firming-up, and congruence

Those various currents are emerging locally. Their emerging, isolated situation exposes them to cognitive distortion: overgeneralisation, dogmatism, delusions of 'golden age' or 'apocalypse'.

For a long time, these currents have developed in ignorance of one another. Increasing effervescence increases the opportunities for

---

[14] Many relevant currents are developing: Sciences of complexity, cognitive science, informatics, neurosciences, science of language, morphogenetics, robotics, design science, sciences of action, psychology, psycho-sociology, socio-anthropology, philosophy of science, epistemology, pragmatism, systemics, constructivism, etc.

pointwise meetings. On such occasions, because they are beholden to individuals, the encounters may turn to confrontation: comparisons, oppositions, self-protection. It is paradoxical that such meetings could bring about an attitude of *defying* rather than *rejoining*. However, these currents remain largely isolated: practitioners do not know researchers; deciders are remote from operators; researchers are partitioned into disciplines.

Emerging currents have not confronted one another: that is, they have not woven links to identify those elements which, beyond their differences, form a common praxis, a striving to transform experience into a conscious science [15].

3 Research on complexity sheds light on the effervescence

Research on complexity provides intelligibility of the effervescence. The paradigm of complexity is being elaborated, relying on concepts made robust by work on epistemology. The following three examples of semantic shift will illustrate the relevance of epistemological roots.

- Shifting *from leader to pilot* points out that persons in charge are no longer able to set up a straight path. Such persons are now more like someone at the wheel, facing the

---

[15] Conscious science is also a sapience, that is, a continuous application of epistemo-ethical critique.

weather and constantly adapting their navigation to bring their ship into harbour,

- Shifting *from optimisation to satisfaction* points up that the implicit assumption of optimisation -- namely that the object under consideration is fully known, closed, independent, with a single criterion for optimisation – is too simplistic for relevance in a continuously evolving context. Especially, this shift emphasizes the requirement to take account of collateral costs which are ignored when considering optimisation of a single objective, whereas objectives themselves are constantly adapting. Nowadays, every decision is made in an uncertain environment, and always according to multiple criteria. We can endeavour to draw on all resources and opportunities – as identified through investigating the contexts and evaluating the stakes – to define a path that is currently satisfactory, aware that any such decision is a wager. At best, optimisation techniques can be a basis for exploratory heuristics,
- Shifting *from theoretician to designer* points up the fact that research is not necessarily an abstracted producer of concepts which are 'true' in themselves. Concepts are now being produced in respect of a project and context that define their conditions of validity.

Research in the field of complex organizational systems is an important trend, though itself a new emergence within the whole of scientific research. These special currents are elaborating conceptual devices for modelling complex systems (*Systems modelling, Systems simulating*) and enabling the exploration of possibilities. These currents in turn can be seen to have several subfields (see Appendix 1)

Thus, it happens that some practice which may seem isolated and tantamount to a cooking recipe may be reconnected through research to a critical epistemological perspective. Conversely, research opens new perspectives on possible practices.

4 Complexity thought leads to identification of new praxes

Modes of thought and action in complexity provide illumination to identify emerging, renewed praxis within the effervescence of society. Some of these praxes are better adapted to some of the challenges. Here are some tentative sketches

- In education, to develop skills in living and learning together,
- In enterprise, to develop co-design of products,
- In ecosystem management, to support adaptive regulation,
- In politics, for co-construction of citizen initiatives.

5 New praxes provide a concrete content to the paradigm of complexity

The paradigm of complexity and associated sciences are often seen as insufficiently concrete for organizations. As a consequence, leaders do not invest the effort required to master its concepts.

Yet the new praxes, which have been widely proven in the field, provide adequate, concrete pathways to shed light on the complex problems faced by those leaders. At all scale levels, these praxes facilitate the intelligibility of multidimensional situations, support the design of new, adapted action strategies, and assist in motivating the collective.

Welcome Complexity: an institutional locus to catalyse the development of our adaptability to evolving context[16]

1 Major challenges for all leaders

Given the current mutation and its challenges to the leaders, there are several well-defined issues in catalysing the diffusion and mastering of praxis:

- Provide relief to those who feel responsible and restore their ability to act;
- Develop leaders' ability to create and maintain a fertile ground and environment for the collective of their subordinates. Such an environment ought to be favourable to the development of each person and to the emergence of pathways appropriate for the problems perceived by the collective;
- Develop an apprenticeship of action and thought in complexity, as well as each person's awareness that they are full-time agents in their collective;
- Anticipate unavoidable crises.

Most leaders are personally aware of those challenges. But so far there is no institution which is free from old practices and able to support, anticipate, clarify and elucidate problems arising, in relationship with those who experience them *in*

---

16 This context itself being transformed by us and conversely transforming us.

situ, as well as developing and disseminating emerging praxes.

2 Work required to address these challenges

The present manifesto is intended to present the issues and the context which may shed light of the mosaic of elements being assembled in the effervescence. It stresses the importance of firmly rooting such concrete elements in Complexity thought. Such elements constitute the daily subject matter of Welcome Complexity.

Boosting the dissemination and mastery of these praxes requires at least three types of work on these concrete elements:

- Building a process for learning a reliable corpus of concepts, practices, methods, approaches, models, all explicitly rooted;
- Practicing these new modes of thought and action in situ, so that leaders can master associated knowledge and skills;
- Personal development of those who apply these practices, to promote 'being with another'.

To master this purpose, readers can consult

- Appendix 2, which includes a list of method elements; and
- Appendix 3 which includes an illustration (Uber) and concrete experiences in past work.

3 The need for a new institution

To carry out this work, there is a need for a locus where emerging threads can be woven together. This locus must be:

- ✓ A **crossroads** where all agents can meet, where links can be woven, praxes consolidated and questions refined to direct research. Welcome Complexity is first of all a meeting place where fruitful surges can be launched, where persons from differing origins can share their desire for renewal, bear witness to their experience and contribute their different insights,
- ✓ An **association** to promote the development of a network of reliable practitioners in the service of transformation,
- ✓ A **lighthouse** illuminating the social effervescence with a benevolent, critical and demanding attitude as a trusted third party,
- ✓ A **workshop** directly connected with the concrete investigation of complex problems; a workspace where leaders can step back with no taboos and conceptualise their life experience with the assistance of theoretical thinkers. This would also contribute to the redesign of professional, business, operational and governance models, as well as of transformation pathways. It would enable the design of new relevant ecosystems (shared platforms,

organizations, rules, modes of value distribution, ...) in response to major societal challenges,

- ✓ An **institute** to disseminate and teach knowledge, as well as develop the practical acquisition of skills. This would support the personal development of leaders and the deep renewal of their conceptual approaches. It would disseminate robust and credible elements on which leaders could rely,
- ✓ A **foundation** to weave all the threads, provide explicit statement and development of praxes, contribute to research by building a corpus and also by formulating a well-articulated, shared semantics,
- ✓ A **watchtower** which would anticipate and take hold of complex problems as they arise now, in order to prepare for upcoming crises. This watch could ask and clarify ethical and civic questions associated with those problems.

Part 3: Conceiving and Self-Conceiving

Introduction

Everywhere in our society there are citizens intent on thinking well.

Such citizens are present among thoughtful practitioners: reflecting on their experience provides for critical rooting and opens new perspectives on action. Welcome Complexity's project is also to facilitate weaving a network among citizens whose thought provides a robust rooting to their action.

To initiate the weaving of this network, this manifesto offers a diagnosis of the context in which we live, as well as high-level shareable objectives. Those objectives can be presented in interlocking phases, starting from the interior life of a citizen who gives attention to epistemology and ethics, and expanding all the way to the life of the city:

- Regenerate our modes of thought and action so they are appropriate to the challenges of transformation in our societies,
- Develop abilities of critical attention for possible contexts of intervention,
- Build pathways adequate to current problems,
- Develop praxis appropriate for these pathways,
- Join what has been disjoined: art, philosophy, sciences,

- Regenerate scientific knowledge in the sense of sapience, i.e., conscious science,
- Through all this, illuminate living-together and acting-together in the city.

As these objectives are being identified, the text will make explicit an understanding of our environment, together with the associated intent. It sketches a possible path, not as an asserted truth, but as a reasonable argument on the ways in which we could reconnect what is today divided.

This renewed weaving of experience, knowledge, skills, is offered as the fertile soil in which we can cultivate and renew the ways we traverse.

Following this manifesto, four Appendices will offer complementary information:

- A brief introduction to complexity,
- Various streams of research in complexity which are still insufficiently connected, as well as other concrete cases of complex situations,
- A beginning of a general diagnosis, with problems which must be addressed in priority to progress to concrete work beyond mere intent,
- The uniqueness of Welcome Complexity, to understand why this project is necessary, given the multiplicity of existing endeavours.

A useful concept: paradigm transition

1 Introduction to the concept of paradigm

The on-going deep transformation of our societies is better understood by applying the notion of transition of an epistemological paradigm[17].

An epistemological paradigm affects the roots of knowledge: what do we call knowledge? How do we build up knowledge? What establishes its validity?

A scientific paradigm fits within an epistemological paradigm, affecting major theories and models: Newtonian paradigm, Electromagnetism, relativistic paradigm, quantum paradigm, etc.

A technological paradigm fits within a scientific paradigm. Observe that the so-called 'digital' transition, often felt to be deep, is itself only a symptom of a deeper one. It aligns with the scientific transition that was induced by quantum mechanics, which made possible the development of information processing technology. The 'digital'

17 A paradigm consists in fundamental principles of association and exclusion ruling every thought and every theory. It forms the roots of our way of representing the world. A paradigm always dwells in the shadow zone or even blind area of our thought. It is what we consider self-evident without ever questioning it. Its principles constitute a belief system which is fruitful and enables a collective to live together in its environment, generation after generation, without needing to call it into question.

transformation is a paradigmatic shift in that it brings about a radical rationalization of previous modes of production, by automating repetitive intellectual processing. This transition in turn occults a deeper epistemological transition, which was not part of previous industrial revolutions: the move from the positivist paradigm to the paradigm of complexity, from focusing on matter-energy objects to information-organisation systems.

2 Our historical, dominant thought paradigm has blind spots

The positivist thought paradigm, which is still dominant among institutions, was formulated by Descartes, who inherited the Platonist tradition rather than the Heraclitan; it was later formalised by Auguste Comte. This paradigm which we label 'classical', is rooted in a dissociation of the subject (*ego cogitans*), from the object (*res extensa*); the subject belongs in metaphysics, while the object belongs in science.

The classical paradigm emerged at the time of the Enlightenment. It was very fruitful and replaced the scholastic approach which was previously dominant. Among its effects, we note that many scientific disciplines, which constitute 'classical' science, are identified by their object. It remains that, like the previous scholastic paradigm, it has its blind spots.

The disjunction of the subject, who engages in the knowledge process, and the object, which is the thing be known, is an essential feature of classical thought. In a more general way, this thought tends to disjoin realities which are not separable, reducing the dimensions of reality: it makes literally inconceivable a connection between realities which have been thus severed; reduction, consisting in examining only one dimension at a time, destroys any complexity in this reality.

This observation may seem abstract and remote, but it shows up in our daily lives. This disjunction-reduction stance is so present, in so many forms, that we have stopped seeing it. Here are four concrete examples:

- Separated disciplinary fields in higher education and research produce blind spots at the intervals between disciplines,
- Sciences of the natural world are called 'hard' sciences, and distinguished from the 'soft' human sciences: this separation is taken for granted,
- The separation between humans and organisations makes it acceptable to effect transformations in organisations without undertaking a transformation of the humans which are their constituents,
- Facts, as methodological constructs, are separated from values in classical science, which eliminates within itself any ethical

> competence, establishing its claim to objectivity by rejecting a connection between scientific knowledge and the subjects that build it. In such a paradigm, responsibility – as belonging in value and not in fact – is considered to make no sense and no science.[18]

Welcome Complexity's project aims at reconnecting what has been disjoined and restoring the complexity of system-objects under scrutiny.

3 There is a need for critical evaluation of the roots of science

When we assume the spectacles of classical science to observe our society, we can only see cause-effect deterministic relationships. This kind of knowledge eliminates any notion of autonomy for individuals or groups, for this would require some degree of indeterminism: the classical outlook excludes individuality, finality, subjecthood.

Thus, the classical paradigm carries a paradox: it excludes from the scope of knowledge the very agency that makes knowledge possible, i.e., the autonomous subject.

---

18 Orthodox economic science reduces phenomena arising in a complex human collective to simple models of a few variables. By this process, it destroys any intelligibility of the phenomena, while claiming, as a science, objectivity with regard to human phenomena that it describes by obliterating subjecthood.

There is now a consensus that scientific theories are not a simple reflection of objective reality: they are coproduced by the structures of the human mind and the sociocultural conditioning of knowledge. Science does not grow simply by a linear accumulation, but transforms itself, regenerating its previous concepts.

The classical paradigm has proven fruitful in furthering an extensive understanding of matter and energy. In that period of fruitfulness, there was no call to criticize the roots of scientific orthodoxy.

Nowadays, however, practices arising from the traditional approach increasingly face resistance, linked to the blind spots of this approach. For instance, an organisation would find it awkward to prescribe that its members should be *autonomous* and creative... We are apparently coming to the end of an era where it was appropriate to protect scientific activity from critical judgment: what was appropriate for science at its origins, when it was marginal and threatened, is no longer so when science is dominant and possibly threatening.

The classical paradigm ended up establishing new dogmas. One of them is that scientific knowledge reflects reality, and that this reality is ruled by universal natural laws. Believers in this dogma receive such laws as the truth about reality, not as constructs rooted in a specific anthropological and social context. For some, this dogma is supported by their need for some absolute truth, just as was the case in the scholastic paradigm. The belief in holding absolute truth brings about a loss of sensitivity to errors in one's system of ideas. Whoever claims to have access to such absolute truth proceeds by dogmatic assertion and gives up on critical deliberation.

Ordinary scientific knowledge obliterates notions of being, existence, integrity, uniqueness, autonomy, intent, ethics, randomness. Such notions dwell in the blind spot of the classical paradigm. The classical scientific approach is exposed to the constant – often actualised – danger of simplifying, flattening, rigidity, closedness, failure to take account of feedback loops. When we accept this diagnosis of the foundation of classical science, we become aware that the way in which human considerations are obliterated in our societies arises, among other origins, from the epistemology underlying classical science.

Starting with this conviction, *Welcome Complexity*'s project watchfully applies critical judgment to the roots of science. This judgement is aimed at shedding light on the shadow zones of the dominant paradigm.

4 By its very root, classical science seems unable to grasp and address the problem of "living well together".

Supposing an intended social objective to be *living and working well together*, it becomes necessary to research fundamental questions about humans, the way they fit in the world and in society, such as: What is a human being? How does it fit in the world of animals, plants, minerals? What is its place in organisations and society?

We feel that the dominant conception of science shows a growing inability to grasp the problems which arise in today's society. At root, this science does not offer suitable concepts to seize those problems.

It follows that classical science cannot respond to the current challenges of *living well together*. Let us be clear: traditional scientific thought is useful, and necessary to address certain kinds of problems. This mode of technical and scientific thought, activating knowledge about *things*, is the reason for the extraordinary efficiency of industrial society.

On the other hand, the paradigm underlying classical science has no concepts to rethink the major societal problems which involve humans. Those parts of reality occulted by the blind spots of the positivist paradigm are literally inconceivable. Applying classical concepts to human relationships, for which they are ineffective, has led to a wrong apperception of human realities.

Inasmuch as the dominant mode of thought cannot conceive of the major societal questions involving humans, it becomes imperative to question it in political, economic and social matters, where it is systematically poor and insufficient.[19]

Welcome Complexity's project is also to address this challenge: not to give up on thinking the system in its totality, and if necessary, contribute to a paradigm in which this totality is conceivable.

5 We notice an effervescence in search of new approaches to current problems

Dominant modes of thought and action appear to be increasing deficient and inadequate to current problems. We observe an emerging effervescence among persons and associations designing and experimenting with new ways to address them. A little attention reveals the profusion of diversely organised collectives (see Appendix 1).

Most such movements are unaware of each other, and do not realise that the work of each of them is a facet of an emerging paradigm,

---

19 'The essence of tyranny is the refusal of complexity' Jakob Burkhardt, Swiss historian

progressively evolving to integrate and transcend the dominant one.

Our project is to connect men and women who are working on these emergences and to facilitate the construction of the paradigm.

6 The deep transformation of our society can be seen as a paradigm transition

There are several characteristic phenomena which convince us that we are living a paradigm transition:

- The coexistence of a declining dominant paradigm and of an emerging, tentative effervescence which progressively builds new ways of thought and action,
- The perception, rather vague, but shared by many, that we are in a post-modern, post-capitalist, post-industrial, post-scientific civilisation: in other words, the almost certainty that our era is finishing, and yet that a desirable future can only be formulated as a vague yearning for a new mode – other modes – of living together,
- Citizens feeling a tension between that which is declining and that which has not yet emerged.

Our project is to illuminate and catalyse this transition.

Developing the new ways of thinking and acting in complexity

1 A project to regenerate the way in which we conduct our thinking

Blind spots in classical modes of thinking keep us from grasping the full complexity of anthropological, social, economic and technical phenomena; we therefore need a renewed method to conduct our thinking rightly. The following constraints apply:

- Be able to distinguish without disjoining or dissociating,
- Respect the features of phenomena which are not well grasped in classical thought, and not mutilate them[20],
- Integrate the interaction between the phenomena and the human subject seeking to understand it.

Our project is to work at renewing the way we conduct our thinking. It is not in complement nor opposition to the classical paradigm. We must integrate and transcend that paradigm into a paradigm of complexity that is able to:

- Distinguish phenomena without separating them, associate them, confront them in search of a fruitful outcome,

20 These features include multidimensionality, multiscale, non-linearity, recursion, dialogic, entanglement, part-randomness, autonomy, emergence;

- Provide conceptual tools to build a knowledge of reality that can be intelligible and transferable without the need to reduce it to elementary units and generic laws,
- Provide intelligibility of self-awareness and articulate it with the interactions experienced by human subjects with others, the world and itself.

2 Transition to complexity is a conceptual challenge

Complexity is a characteristic attributed to the whole of our perceptions and interpretations. It is a way of understanding the world in which we have our being. It is the awareness that there is so much we do not know about this world, and that our knowledge itself is just a collection of reasonable hypotheses in the current context and may evolve over time.

The classical thought paradigm arose through deep disjunctions, which affect our ways of thinking and acting. These disjunctions have dug deep furrows in our thinking:

- In philosophy: object-subject, *de facto-de jure*, substance-essence, innate-acquired, freedom-necessity, change-identity, negation-deprivation, content-modality, unique-universal,
- In science: nature-culture, practice-theory, one-multiple, micro-macro, internal-external, structure-function, order-disorder,

homogenous-heterogenous, dependency-autonomy, producer-product, *ex ante-ex post*, cause-effect.

To regenerate our ways of thinking and develop a paradigm of complexity is to face a conceptual challenge and re-examine the formal logic which is our current guide. We are challenged to integrate and transcend our conceptual boundaries and accept those polarities without separating their polar terms.

Our project is also to extend a collective invitation to this undertaking, which, while well initiated, has yet to become satisfactory.

3 A constraint and a requirement for this project: questioning our language

The 'realities' among which we live, and of which we are a part, must always be more complex than the language we use to grasp them. Language is a means for building knowledge of reality, yet it also is a medium which occults that which it claims to represent. There is always a tendency to confuse the word and the reality is represents.

Our project is also a constant questioning of the relationship of words to things, to resist this tendency.

4 A constraint and a requirement for this project: to apply this way of thinking to specific, multi-dimensional problem situations

Conducting one's thinking well requires formulating a more refined epistemology, taking account of the way in which knowledge is produced, in order to prepare regenerated modes of thought. One likely valuable approach to this work is to stand back and review the roots of western thought.

Old modes of thought and action affect this conceptual work with a permanent risk: that of dissociating thought from action. Epistemological work is not disembodied. To be relevant, it must constantly connect thought and action. Epistemology is constructed and refined in connection with concrete activities of knowledge production; therefore, it must consider the content of knowledge itself. The work must ensure that research is conscious of its own premises: choosing a method already involves a social choice.

As we see it, the emerging paradigm of complexity cannot be a theory of everything. It is a guide for the exercise of thought in concrete situations. In contact with constraints of reality, epistemological work eschews the danger of becoming a speculative, disconnected abstraction. It also escapes the risk of aporia, being subjected to unanticipated, deep social changes and merely react to them.

Our project is to put in practice this way of thinking on problems arising here and now, which need to be investigated. This implies a tireless shuttling between concrete daily practice and the roots of this way of thinking and acting. We must confront this way of thinking with perceived realities, produce concrete knowledge, and feedback onto a refinement of epistemology. While polar opposites, epistemology and practice are indivisible.

5 An intentionally conscious journey is probably needed for transition to complexIty

A person trained in ways of thinking rooted in positivism had the assurance that they would formulate universal laws. This rooting was very reassuring, existentially, for anyone seeking absolute truths.

On the opposite, taking on complexity brings on anxiety, as it radically brings back uncertainty. A person seeing the world as complex realizes that any constructed 'truth' is biodegradable. Any 'truth' is dependent on the soil that nurtured it, of its conditions of formation and existence. Any theory is refutable. In this perspective, a truth is not defined in opposition to error, but in relation to life and to its adaptation to the authoring subject.

Working on a new way of thinking and acting again raises the root questions on the human condition, which are the source of both existential anguish and wonderment. Yet is the anxiety of radical uncertainty greater than the cold certainty of death? Does it not make it possible to renew our conception of each person's life, freedom and ethical responsibility?

The quest for knowledge takes us to the limits of what can be conceived and formulated. We believe that in order to reopen the human domain, we are to assume a thoughtful pragmatism, in whatever form it takes. The paradigm of complexity restores autonomy, freedom, responsibility,[21] the potential for genuine joy, all of these inseparable from the anguish that we must face.

Assuming that paradigm transition, as experienced by each of us, includes an existential dimension, this dimension is the most difficult obstacle to the transition. Our project watches for means of relieving such anguish, both by a kindly attention to others and by making clear the

---

21 Progress in cognitive neuroscience increasingly stresses the non-existence of free will on the basis of the huge weight of decisions made in a stimulus-response dynamic. No free will does not mean no autonomy for a thinking subject: neuroscience observes that human brain and nervous system are complex systems with unpredictable chaotic regimes. A subject's thought system is able to meta-systemise itself – i.e., adopt a new viewpoint enabling it to articulate theretofore disjoint perspectives – through reflecting on its own thoughts. This reinforces the challenge and the importance for a human subject to think itself in complexity in its interaction with the world, to overcome the trends to mechanization, instrumentalization and objectivation.

avenues offered to anyone with the courage of undertaking the transition.

6 Opening up with the emerging paradigm

The paradigm of complexity is opening a path to a renewal of our domains of knowledge. It enables us to reach intelligibility of phenomena well beyond what we thought were our limits. Where the classical paradigm cuts abruptly, the paradigm of complexity spreads a sfumato[22] sliding from the most obvious idea to complete obscurity, through the whole gamut of vagueness.

The emerging way of thought can formalise a transferable knowledge, not absolute but associated with a given context and project.

The paradigm of complexity re-establishes science as a quest, which is not separable from a subject, and produces constructs which do not claim to reflect reality. This quest is a construction in progress, like a path, with potential to stray; it feels its way along.

The paradigm of complexity invites us to organise statements as signposts on a path that is always in construction. Such statements address a process, a flow, a life of things, rather than some attributes that would characterize an object and define it as an object of study. They are respectful of the dimensions of reality, particularly the

---

[22] *Sfumato*: This term refers to the vaporous effect that Leonardo da Vinci affected in his paintings, creating a soft form with imprecise outlines.

unpredictable nature of the systems about which we are developing some knowledge. This paradigm opens, restores and renews our perspectives.

7 The paradigm of complexity restores freedom of thought by eschewing simplistic thinking and "solutionism"

Traditional ways of thinking and acting, still common today, represent a constant danger for the project. We have mentioned the pressure to dissociate thought from action. There is also the pressure to believe in universal solutions.

Those who have already transitioned to a paradigm of complexity will consider it self-evident; but it is worth writing for those who, aspiring to it, are still penetrated with the classical paradigm: those new ways of thinking and acting are not a martingale, nor are they the Grail. They do not bring a meta-solution that could untangle problems without scrutinizing the details where the devil dwells. They are not a *superior* mode of thought.

Rather, the paradigm of complexity is a *passage to open reason* which enables us to take back a conceptual freedom from the classical paradigm, and yet not exclude it from use in the phases of heuristic exploration. It articulates and conjoins what the classical paradigm would separate: it calls into question the premises which the classical paradigm takes for granted. It is a metaphorical fountain of youth in which we see the same objects in a new way.[23] It is a more intelligent way of studying the same problem by means of a new description.

8 Developing a praxis anchored on concrete problems

The practical application of thinking in complexity is a journey made up of back and forth navigation of the phenomenon, seen as a system. It requires a pragmatic anchoring of work on what exists concretely.

The general intent of *Welcome Complexity* is to implement a *working-together* in effective, problem-rich situations, with the following worksites:

- Commit to a collective elucidation of issues, contexts and stakeholders in tangled problem situations;
- Work on designing regenerated processes and pathways rather than apply preformatted resolution methods;
- Recover the ways of a multidimensional thought, integrating and developing formalisation and quantification, but not bound by them;
- Commit to describing phenomena to the point of making their uniqueness explicit;

---

[23] *"We have always treated systems as if they were objects; it is time to think of objects as systems"* Edgar Morin, La Méthode

- Accept that we do not know the extent of our ignorance, and be open to the mystery of self and the world;
- Constantly pay attention to ethical issues in the context of our approaches.

Building new pathways in a constantly evolving context

1 The challenges of practicing open reason: to open perspectives and possible pathways

Our leaders are immersed in a constantly evolving context and are perplexed.[24] We observe that they are aware that scientific approaches do not fit their living experience. They know that regardless of the scale level, those approaches cannot support the design and transformation of the organisations which they lead. On the whole, they realize that such approaches, no matter how sophisticated, are ultimately dependent on the formulation of the problems. They know that all the data presented in support of conclusions are conditioned by those initial formulations. But, lacking reliable alternatives, they make do, by 'triangulation', and use available means as heuristic devices.

---

24 Listening to the community of leaders, we hear: how can we survive in a globalized environment? How do we preserve employment and regulations and still compete? How do we adapt to the digital revolution? Where is the next disruption coming from? How do we select a model? How do we speed up? How do we make our organisation more agile?
Listening to the political community, we hear: how do we prevent the rise of extremism? How do we reserve some leeway under our budget constraints? Where are the deep levers to act on society? How do we restore political over against lobbies and industrial complexes?

The concepts of the paradigm of complexity bring a fundamental renewal to our outlook and support the opening of new perspectives on current problems, as soon as we draw on them to elucidate the challenges and investigate our questions in an evolving situation.

Our project is to stay related to effective situations as experienced by leaders as problems for which traditional approaches do not offer satisfactory pathways.

In the current transition, we can discern, among others, several classes of issues which arise in the thinking of leaders:

- Redesign of modes of production in a rapidly changing context,
- Dialogue among expert domains,
- Adaptability of organisations,
- Cultural transition,
- Positioning of an organisation in its ecosystem,
- Awareness of one's place in the environment,
- Redesign of organisational ecosystems.

2 A deeply felt need to redesign the modes of production

In every sector, large-scale modes of mass production have been so far guided by a logic of programming and quantification, replacing humans with machines. Such guiding logic is losing steam.

As the context evolves, modes of production, in every sector,[25] are being transformed into more adequate modes, which abandon this logic of industrial programming. Emerging modes of production, in the field, are introducing renewed logics which can be clearly illuminated by the paradigm of complexity.

Conversely, these concepts provide for the design of renewed approaches, adapted for the unique, evolving problems of each organisation. Among these concepts: autonomy of human beings, old[26] and new rhetorics, coupling of systems, multi-scale logics, such principles as dialogic, hologrammatic, recursive, self-balancing, accommodation/assimilation, articulating of opposites, synergy/co-operation and antagonism/competition, genetic algorithms, multi-agent simulations, etc.

---

[25] This transition affects every sector as defined in the framework of the classical paradigm : health, transportation, education, armed forces, building construction, energy, etc.

[26] The Greek metis (μητις), a strategy of the relationship to others and the world which relies on CUNNING, is a form of thought and intelligence, a mode of knowledge. It engages a complex, coherent set of mental stances and intellectual behaviour combining flair, acumen, precision, mental flexibility, resourcefulness, watchfulness, a sense of opportunity, a variety of skills, and long experience. It is multiple, polymorphous, and tackles realities which are fleeting, fluid and perplexing.

Welcome Complexity's project is to research this redesign of modes of production, insisting on working to understand, and understanding to work.

3 Developing a dialog among men and women endowed with differing expertise and experience

We daily note that our inherited modes of organisation have often brought about *silos*[27] i.e., human groups which are closed to each other, although dedicated to the same ends.

Our current questions are multidimensional; for each dimension of a problem we need specific approach logics, which take time to acquire.

The transformation of a multidimensional system requires a dialog among humans who have developed distinct and complementary masteries. In each participant, such dialog produces a shared knowledge, which is the more felicitous as the knowledge was dispersed and fragmented. In this dialog each person can step sideways out of their established thought patterns.

A collective needs relevant orchestration of interactions among dialoguing actors who each carry different logics. A conjugation of these approaches can provide intelligent orientation to

---

[27] This label simultaneously evokes the nutritive potential of the contents, the smooth, closed reserve of the container, and a vertical integration which ignores lateral connections.

the behaviour of the organisation of this collective[28], in pursuit of its adopted calling.

In the field, we have observed that this orchestration can emerge as an appropriate practice at any scale level. *Welcome Complexity's* project is to develop and disseminate the praxis of *dialogue* among different viewpoints.

4 Developing organisations' adaptability to evolving contexts

We daily note that the practice of planning and programming by reverse engineering fails when the context evolves, in an increasingly complex and rapid manner. This calls into question the programmatic stance.

We discover once again that any human action, from its inception, escapes the control of its initiator and engages in the multiple interactions of society, which subvert it from its intent and reorient it contrary to the original aim.

The more complex the situation, the faster the obsolescence of classical strategies, hence the expanding failure of classical approaches, including decision-action dichotomy, indiscriminate application of actions, blindness to failure to obtain desired results.

The emerging paradigm acknowledges the ecology and time-binding of an action, the

---

28 Such an organisation of a collective is termed a collective action system.

fundamentally adaptive nature of any transformation effort, the need to take into account the process of rebalancing in systems, to identify positive feedback loops and to adjust actions to the belief structures of each person in a given time and context.

As to governance of organisations, a transition requires pragmatism – in the philosophical sense. Pragmatism does not make claim to objectivity – which makes no practical sense. Pragmatic behaviour gives close consideration to its immediate consequences. It adjusts itself constantly in contact and interaction with the environment.

In this transition, governance no longer relies on objective, rational and programmed strategy, but rather on a projective action strategy. This action strategy often is a reactive, swift, conscious adaptation, both of the organisation and of intended action plans. "Here a complex mode of thought extends into a complex mode of action"[29]

Welcome Complexity's project is to develop and disseminate patterns for the elaboration of projective action strategies, at all scale levels, in the context of effective projects in organisations. "Complexity calls for strategy".[30]

---

[29] In Edgar Morin 'Science avec Conscience', (Fayard, 1982) p.318

[30] *"Complexity calls for strategy. Only strategy supports progress in uncertainty and randomness [...] (it) is the art of making use of information as it arises in action, integrating it, instantly formulating*

5 Catalysing the cultural transition

As we read the context, one major challenge of the current transition is to enable every person to transition from a culture where they apply a program set from above – causing instrumentalization and loss of personal responsibility – to a culture of *ingenium* with autonomy at every scale – that of the handyman, the designer, the engineer, the architect, the artist.

This is a powerful transition in behaviour, and in the way one relates to one's sovereignty. It has an existential component of relating to the human condition:

- The person in a role of operator must pass from execution to entrepreneurship, recover their sovereignty from the hierarchy, make use of critical thought, develop their interactive autonomy and resume awareness of their share in responsibility;
- The person in a role of leader must pass from direction to governance, delegate some of their power, trust others, while remaining watchful of the process leading to decision;
- The person in a role of expert must pass from owning an immutable truth to on-

---

patterns of action and assembling as much certainty as possible to face uncertainty" Edgar Morin, Science avec Conscience, 1990

going adaptation of concepts to the evolving context.

Welcome Complexity's project is to catalyse this cultural transition in each person.

6 Fitting the organisation in its environment

Current organisations are faced with another large family of problems: fitting in one's environment in such a way that ecological constraints are integrated within the very operation of the organisation.

In this transition, an organisation moves from ignoring its impact to integrating and assuming that impact at all levels of internal operation. It requires a deep redesign of governance and organisation. The project is to contribute to modes of thought and action that fit this intent.

Welcome Complexity's project is to foster organisations taking account of their interaction with their environment.

7 Awareness of one's position in the environment

An organisation can assume and integrate its position in the environment only to the extent that its human members think and act in awareness of such interaction. For the organisations in which we take part to assume the environment, we need a path for each of us, internally, to:

- Leave the classical paradigm that disjoins nature from culture, individual from environment;
- Develop humility and acknowledge that we are ignorant of what we don't know;
- Develop responsibility for the impacts of our actions, whether personal or through some organisation.

8 Redesigning the ecosystem of organisations

While organisations must adapt to a new context, perceived as an external constraint, civic responsibility demands that we reflect on adapting the context itself, which is the result of our collective construction. Human societies, and their cultures, bring about contexts which may or may not favour this or that form of life. They may suffer these contexts as a fatality and only think of adapting to them. They may also, with more ambition, envision the possibility of acting on the contexts themselves.

Welcome Complexity's project is to support the redesign of contexts, i.e., of the ecosystems in which organisations are inserted.

Developing a praxis that is adapted for the new pathways

1 Introduction

Building new pathways requires a new praxis. Everyone faces the challenge to acquire it. In the situations we experience, we are questing subjects, seeking, experiencing, feeling our way, dialoguing and co-constructing with others. In such situations:

- Past experience is not a clear, unequivocal source of knowledge,
- Adapting one's action can be effective without an a priori clear conceptualisation and knowledge,
- Knowledge does not consist in the piling up of data or information, but in organising incomplete information around an intent.

The emerging praxis consists in making full use of the qualities of a subject in their existence, relying on the complete resources of reason.

2 Restoring a readiness to be creative and to make mistakes

The classical paradigm promotes temptations: that of command and control, which limit autonomy and creativity, that of certainty, which denies the possibility of error, that of disjunction, which rejects opposites. Deterministic classical thought seeks to reduce randomness and mistakes to mere deviations from a reference which remains absolute. So classical thought seeks to eliminate them as anomalies.

Observing history makes it clear that so-called 'errors' have played a major role. Also, the fate of organisations, at any scale, depends on 'errors' in understanding a situation. Accordingly, making mistakes is not in itself serious for an organisation. What is serious is blindness and passivity in the face of events which are deemed insignificant whereas they are in fact critical. This happens when deciders fail to grasp the meaning of such events and end up making inadequate decisions.

At all scale levels, lack of awareness, critical thought, commitment, adaptability, self-limitation, is tantamount to poverty and degeneration, and may lead to symbolic or real death.

Our project consists in restoring the ability for creativity and error through a logic of trial and error, to develop attention to the evolution of the environment and the ability to evaluate the significance of events.

This is a major challenge in a period of transition when leaders are short of clues for distinguishing what is essential from what is incidental, and when caution and immobility win over courage and willingness to attempt. There lies a serious risk for the collective to lose its way.

3 Developing the palette of open reason

The emerging paradigm develops in its practitioner a palette of *open reason*. This is the name we give to a form of rationality that eschews rationalization, a regenerated rationality that applies critical thought to the principles of formal rationality. It could be characterized as follows:

- Alert awareness of the conscious significance of events,
- Awareness of the limits of the model used to understand phenomena,
- Awareness of the limits of reason itself,
- Sensitivity to randomness and disorder[31],
- Sensitivity to unique, original and historic features of phenomena, which cannot be accounted for by general laws,
- Integrating the relationship of a subject to an object in the knowledge that the subject has of the object,
- Integrating the questions of existence, being, and the psychic-physical relationship,
- Commitment to critical deliberation.

As compared to classical praxis, the emerging praxis prefers examination to analysis, conjunction to separation, possibilities to

---

31 Manifested in serendipity, which consists in finding something other than what one was looking for

necessities, proscriptive[32] to prescriptive stance, regularities and constraints to laws, *organising* to organisation, asking the question to finding the solution, a will to know to a will to manipulate.

In the emerging praxis, the end is never a given, hence method cannot take precedence over critical review. The approaches of this praxis re-establish a subject in its two polarities: it is as prepared to receive and be transformed as to emit and transform.

The palette of open reason develops upon each opportunity to listen openly to persons who are different from oneself, including, even especially, when such persons do not wield an authority that would give *a priori* legitimacy to their discourse.

Welcome Complexity's project is to facilitate for each person access to the new ways of thought in complexity.

4 Developing the practice of critical deliberation based on credible arguments

In the effort to think well, there is a first step that is often useful: deconstructing false certainties and pseudo-answers, to reopen a field of possibilities. The new praxis is bound up with

32 In the proscriptive stance, whatever is not explicitly forbidden is permitted. The proscriptive stance states explicitly what is forbidden: it pertains to necessity. In the prescriptive stance, whatever is not explicitly permitted is forbidden. The prescriptive stance states explicitly what is permitted: it pertains to obligation.

the ability to step sideways from one's own certainties and understand another's viewpoint, to gain new reaches without giving up one's own viewpoint.

This praxis leads to a way of listening to stakeholders that is free of those hierarchical relationships which we carry with us, consciously or not (social status, competence and skills, origin, etc.) and that acknowledges the value of each human experience.

This movement has an existential component: whoever takes this path may have to let go of their certainties, in their inner journey.

In the effort to think well, it is not necessary to limit one's reason to Aristotelian syllogisms. Any form of reasoning is licit. The only constraint is that one's arguments should be credible and that one should be accepting of equally credible counterarguments, in a critical deliberation. This art is a new rhetoric.

Welcome Complexity's project is to develop the use of open reason and the new rhetoric based on credible arguments and critical deliberation.

5 Developing the practice of "meta-method"

We consider reflection to be the richest characteristic of thought, able to work at a metalevel (to metasystemize[33]) and to transcend

---

[33] Passing to a metalevel must be distinguished from transcending. Passing to meta concerns cognitive relationships: I work in arithmetic,

itself[34]: this is the feature of thought which can overcome a closed set of alternatives in a given paradigm, and provide them with a richer context in which new, previously inconceivable alternatives may emerge. In this view, reflection ought not to be as it is today: this is not a property of philosophy.

Meta-method consists in exercising this rich feature of thought. It has two aspects:

- Mental duality consists in viewing a system simultaneously as a pattern of components and a pattern of relationships. These two outlooks form a duality, in that they are both complementary and mutually irreducible,
- Passing to meta consists in taking up a new viewpoint from which it is possible to

---

then I consider the limits of arithmetic thought (Gödel). Or, I calculate, then I consider the limits of calculation (Turing, Church). Within the context of mathematics, Grothendiek has initiated Category theory, placing all of mathematics into a richer context where there appear previously inconceivable links between analysis, algebra and geometry. In a less ambitious way, still within mathematics, the resolution of this elementary enigma X2 = -1, is another example of a system going beyond itself: from a conceptual impossibility in the real domain, it resolves itself by an extension to a new (complex) space. Passing to a metalevel can be done without questioning the epistemological paradigm.

34 Transcendence applies to ontological relationships, i.e., those between 'hard' scientific concepts and more encompassing, if les precise, notions: I define entropy in thermodynamics, then I generalize the concept to any system. I build holograms (by Laplace transform) then I envision brain activity as holographic.

articulate the intelligibility of two aspects that were heretofore disjointed.

We need to develop a praxis that will not be fragmented into contradictions and antagonisms, but create a new conjunction within which such antagonisms, while keeping their destructive features, will also develop constructive potential.

Welcome Complexity's project is to develop both formalisation and practice of meta-method.

6 Developing the practice of conscious collective emergences

The practice of meta-method is crucially important with respect to the needs identified in organisations.

One way to think of a human collective is to create a model in which each subject is seen as a component of complex system kind. In this way of thinking, a passage to meta may provide for the apparently irreducible antagonisms from each subject are integrated and overcome; they become conceivable from a new, shared viewpoint. Thus, meta-method:

- Develops sensitivity to such collective emergences,
- Allows each individual to step sideways from their self-referring logic,
- Allows individuals to start thinking of the collective of which they are a component,

- Makes us receptive to new skills, i.e., conceive of and consciously animate such collective emergences.

Welcome Complexity's project is to develop the design of processes aimed at bringing about such emergences and the practice of in situ animation at each stage of the process.

Conjoining again what has been disjoined

1 Introduction

The paradigm of complexity acknowledges that uniqueness, randomness, autonomy, are irreducible aspects of phenomena as experienced and perceived by anyone.

Given this renewed perspective, formal logic loses its absolute validity, any theory is always open and unfinished, society and culture allow us to question science, instead of contributing to belief taboos. Our relationship to the world is hereby renewed: it can integrate all those aspects, without giving up on building a scientific, transferable form of knowledge. This new relationship to the world takes account of every activity of humans interacting with their environment. Instead of excluding, it conjoins the scientist, the philosopher and the artist.

Welcome Complexity's project is to traverse a path of regenerations for this relationship among domains which were heretofore dissociated by the dominant paradigm of separation-exclusion. We must conjoin again, concretely. We must embody a renewed dialog among science, art, philosophy, society and the world.

2 Connecting science, art and philosophy

2.1 *Conjoining art and science*

Art can be seen as a practice in which a unique piece of work expresses the perception of a meaning by an active being; as such, it demands that this being should be continuously present and aware of itself and of the world; this awareness turns this whole being into a conjunction of the meaning being expressed and the piece of work being shaped.

The discipline of an artist – such few who are genuine – seems even more demanding than the logician's, which mostly involves mental work, whereas an artist's engages the whole being.

Scientific creation takes from art discipline this demanding, hesitant search for other possibles. In both disciplines we find a conjunction of open exploration and rigorous selection. We find an instructive example in Leonardo da Vinci's *disegno*[35] which he exercised equally as an artist, a philosopher and a scientist.

2.2 *Conjoining science and philosophy*

The special characteristic of philosophy is its reflexiveness, in which a subject turns back on itself. The special characteristic of science is its insistence on verification, of the reproducibility and falsification of theory, i.e., on its ability to prove itself wrong.

---

35 Da Vinci describes disegno as purposeful drawing. *"Disegno is so excellent that it not only displays the work of nature, but produces an infinitely greater variety. It goes beyond nature because elementary natural forms are limited, whereas the forms that a human eye demands from human hands are without limit."* Leonardo da Vinci, Notebooks

On the whole, scientific thought is still short of thinking itself through, of examining its own path and its own ambivalence. It has always relied on philosophy for its premises. So, there is no boundary between science and philosophy when we trace back to the roots of science.

Philosophical logic, underlying its critical discourse, is as rigorous as scientific logic, although of a wider extent. Logical rigour does not justify a boundary between science and philosophy. Yet modern philosophy runs on empty, because it does not address the objects of empirical knowledge.

It seems to us that the true philosophers of our era are those rare scientists who take time to reflect and deliberate on science, or those rare philosophers who work on thinking about science and associated practices. In the elaboration of quantum mechanics, a high point of philosophical reflection in modern humanity was the public debate between Niels Bohr and Albert Einstein on the nature of reality. Major scientific problems are major philosophical problems, for which experiment provides new formulations.

Knowing scientific knowledge necessarily includes a dimension of reflection which cannot be delegated to philosophy in isolation. Restoring a critical dialog between science and philosophy, open and to the benefit of both, is an integral part of the emerging method for thinking well.

The positivist paradigm has seen an impressive progress of scientific certainty, and by the same token an impressive growth of uncertainty: in the shadow of its certainties, science gives rise to a vast array of questions which it might wish to bypass. And beyond such formulated questions, we are naturally ignorant of what is missing to our knowledge.

At the locus outlined by what we think we know and by what we are aware of not knowing, there can arise a fruitful dialog with philosophy on fundamental problems of humanity – ontological, epistemological, ethical and eschatological.

2.3 *Conjoining science, art and philosophy*

In the paradigm of complexity, it becomes apparent that art, science and philosophy have a common spirit: they share in a demanding and rigorous judgement in command of thought and action.

Science has in great measure separated from art and philosophy when establishing itself; yet the only difference is that the means for verification and refutation of scientific work are more immediate and effective.

Welcome Complexity's project is to revive the dialog among art, philosophy and science.

3 Reconnecting science, politics and society

3.1 *Reconnecting science and society*

It is generally accepted now that scientific work is not disembodied. Science is living stuff that keeps evolving, in which a dialog develops between subject and object, between social anthropology and natural science.

We feel the need to break the insularity of science and terminate the separation between science and society, while maintaining some degree of autonomy as necessary for research.

3.2 *Developing a science consciously connected to its society*

In relation to art and philosophy self-aware science needs a science of science, a knowledge of knowledge. To follow its own way, science must acquire an epistemological perspective. This perspective, which can make visible the rooting of science in culture and society, would reveal metaphysical postulates and even a mythology hiding inside scientific activity.

3.3 *Restoring scientists' ethical responsibility*

In the paradigm of complexity, facts as methodological constructs and *values* as what is worthwhile are conjoined, in the same way as science and the society in which it has its roots.

As science at its beginnings needed to isolate itself from the rest of society – to remain fruitful and eschew religious dogma – similarly for each researcher the knowledge imperative had to become an absolute of their ethos – to overcome all limitations in the search for knowledge. This imperative subsists in our society as ideological remnants, such as the myth of the hero, risking life to bring about the triumph of scientific truth over dogma. Such is Galileo.

Given current issues, both ethical and civic, in research, it is necessary to end this domination of the ethical stance, prevalent in current scientific circles, that *disinterested* knowledge is above any other value. We must establish a critical deliberation which takes account of all civic issues in any scientific work.

3.4 *Developing a society able to orient science*

As we see it, science is an organic process, not a possessor of some special truth, but proponent of currently acceptable explanations, sustained by an intersubjective consensus in the scientific community. It is stuff in evolution.

If, to ensure dynamism and fruitfulness, science must embody and assume a mosaic of values, it cannot be independent from some form of civic governance, which needs definition.

Non-sovereign powers tend to orient and use research for ends which have not been scrutinized in open civic dialog. Such science is directed to some application through a logic that is too short-term in the context of society, and often ignores the diversity of paths and viewpoints. Civic governance would set up limits to safeguard such research *and also* ensure that researchers are clearly conscious of their ethical and epistemological choices.

Welcome Complexity's project is to connect scientists and citizens. We must ensure a well-argued ethical debate about science, to contribute light to politics and civil society. We must provide a form of scientific education that does not avoid critical work, and no longer conveys some latent epistemology that settles as dogma and blocks creative, critical thought.

4 Connecting reason, action and the sense of existence

We have mentioned the existential dimension of this project several times. We now sketch the relationships we offer among reason, action and the sense of existence.

4.1 *Between reason and the sense of existence*

We believe that existence and being are neither rational nor irrational: they just are. Reality always transcends such a distinction. Though we can, by meditation, achieve a metaphysical apprehension on the essence of being, we shall never have a rational knowledge of being and of existence as such.

Reason, as developed within the paradigm of complexity, acknowledges what classical reason repressed. It maintains a dialog between the rational and the irrational (the absurd), *and also* with the a-rational and the super-rational. It does not accept being shut in some opposition between what might be termed rational and what might not. The reason of true rationality converses with what is unrationalizable, unpredictable, disorderly, unknown, and does not obliterate those things. Among other things, it maintains a dialog with emotions, feelings, dreams, mystery, as so many springs and resources.

4.2 *Between reason and world-facing strategy*

We believe that every human being is manifested by their end-seeking action in the world, with tools as intermediates. Humans explore, attempt, act while seeking. Tools may impose constraints, but not a program. Humans are philosophers, they reflect on their action. They think, design, steer and handle tools. Rationality thus shows up as a strategy for knowledge and action.

Rationality depends on the development of autonomous thought, i.e., the ability to perceive, understand and use multiple dependencies while going beyond them – in tools, structures, ideologies, etc.

Rationality as strategy is a dialog with the world, a struggle and co-operation with disorder, endeavouring to make it intelligible. Strategy, in general, is thinking and acting in complexity.

4.3 *Between sense of existence and other-facing strategy*

To begin with, we note that the sense of existence is experienced: it cannot be proven. A person's sense of existence also depends on the consideration granted by others. In relating to others, what grants existence is an authentic relating, i.e., one in which the other is not seen as an object susceptible of manipulation but as a subject whose freedom we respect.

4.4 *Between sense of existence and self-facing strategy*

The sense of existence also arises from an authentic relating to oneself as if it were other, the not seeing oneself as an object susceptible of manipulation, the acknowledgement of one's own share of creation, unknown and mystery. Regardless of the form of their action in the world, independently of any theory, humans, it appears, must be acknowledged as *self-poets*, inasmuch as at least in part they create and are creators of their own uniqueness (*autopoiesis*).

Welcome Complexity's project is to develop each person's sense of existence, through the quality of the strategy of knowledge and action within each of us in relationship to self, others and the world.

Connecting humans with the planet

Inasmuch as humans have an effect on the planet, and as the planet has a feedback effect on humans, and because this human action is collective, any account of the so-called natural ecology (minerals, animals, plants) must include the collective action of humans which transforms the planet. Humans and the planet are interdependent and relatively autonomous. The study of 'natural' phenomena cannot be divorced from 'human' phenomena.

In the emerging paradigm, design and action take place in full awareness of this co-dependency between humans and their environment, between what they produce and what produces them, between self and other.

Welcome Complexity's project is to develop each organisation's ability to see itself as a respectful guest, relating codependently with the environment.

Building the new scientific knowledge

1 Developing the roots of the new scientific knowledge

1.1 *Extending the domain of the knowable, and illuminating blind spots*

We have argued that the field of knowledge accessible to the classical paradigm is limited: the classical method can only conceive of causality external to objects. In the classical approach there is no conceptual space of randomness, uniqueness, autonomy, self, and a fortiori subjects and life. In phenomena, the classical paradigm allows us to see only quantities or objects susceptible of manipulation, where exist beings and individuals.

The classical paradigm simply excludes from the domain of the knowable what it cannot conceive. In that paradigm, some sciences are marginalised as 'heterodox', or 'soft', in opposition to the 'hard' or 'orthodox' domains. The domination of this paradigm is so strong that it has caused a scission of communities within some disciplines – e.g., sociologists or economists – into two families: one that claims to be 'scientific', the other resisting such 'scientificisation'.

The searchlight beam of the classical paradigm covers only a part of 'reality'. Those streams of activity so far excluded by dominant science as 'heterodox' have endeavoured not to neglect essential parts of 'reality'. They have maintained the ideas of autonomy, randomness, uniqueness, historicity, subjecthood. They have made some way forward outside of the classical paradigm.

The emerging scientific paradigm elaborates scientific roots for those concepts. It opens the potential for integration, transcending the ortho-hetero dichotomy, by giving roots to all of science within a new paradigm where old and new concepts create a new domain of the knowable.

In this new scope, it becomes possible to give recognition, root and support to individual and collective aspirations to autonomy and freedom, which were excluded from the field of knowledge. One may begin to consider a science of autonomy.

This transition has conditions: we must give up on the scale of measurement – which is limited to the matter-energy layer – and acknowledge that in the information-organisation layer everything is about change of form.

1.2 *Being open to every kind of rationality*

As we follow this path we are building, we begin to glimpse a new kind of rationality. Classical rationality was seeking an expected static order in nature. The emerging rationality endeavours to conceive of an expected dynamic and adaptive organisation, and of existence. To achieve some intelligibility of the world, we cannot be restricted to a rationality that only fits physics.[36] Other disciplines – biology, neurophysiology, neurobiology, ecology, informatics, cybernetics, robotics, cognitive sciences, communication sciences, linguistics, psychology, socio-anthropology, philosophy – all contribute to this emerging new rationality.

This new rationality shapes scientific concepts which were not conceivable in the classical paradigm: autonomy, self, individuality, subjecthood, freedom, uniqueness, randomness, history.

---

36 What the reader may consider self-evident is unfortunately not what we observe in institutions. Take the example of economics: this discipline has for decades striven to set itself up along the lines of Newtonian physics. In the past 15 years we have noticed that it is attempting to renew itself. It is questioning some of its postulates on 'individual' behaviour, taking more inspiration from cognitive science and psychosociology. However, such borrowings have not yet led it to give up, or even question, its insistence on formalising according to classical rationality: this, in spite of the closer affinity of economics with life sciences than with physics. Both study the deployment of life around concepts of resources, consumption, stocks and fluxes, autonomous organisations and their environment.

Along this path, concepts are no longer substantive notions, nor are they metaphysics or principles. We begin to think of autonomy, the individual, the subject, not as metaphysical notions but as rooted and conditioned physically, biologically and socially. So, for instance it becomes possible to give a scientific sense to the notion of autonomy.

The intelligibility that we develop about such realities as they are becoming knowable does not provide for control over them; on the other hand, it assists our thinking to guide our action in complexity, by changing our outlook:

- We were observing through the prism of natural laws as they apply to matter and energy; now we acquire ways of conceiving the dynamics of information and organisation,
- We were in search of reduced elements, such as a skeleton or a structure, and investigated their laws and constraints with the purpose of manipulating them; now we find means to think of an element in its connectivity, with its flesh and its environment,
- We thought in terms of irreducible opposites; now we find means to conceive the interaction and association of determinism and freedom, of autonomy and dependency: freedom is constrained by the conditions of its emergence, but it can react

on these conditions and bring about autonomy.

Welcome Complexity's project is to contribute to the development of the paradigm of complexity.

There is much at stake. The form of current organisations is still by and large majority founded arbitrarily on power and territory. The challenge is to provide conceptual tools to support *sapient* thinking[37] about organisation and governance, so that all organisations serve the collective's objectives optimally.

This project of a scientific contribution is inseparable from concrete work in the design of organisations.

In the emerging paradigm, the term *sapient* is being substituted to the term *scientific*, which is too strongly associated with a reductionist stance.

2 Articulating scientific disciplines which were disconnected before

2.1 *Linking major disciplines*

The positivist paradigm as formalised by Auguste Comte brought about a linear view in the organisation of the system of sciences. Sciences

---

37 SAPIENCE, or "conscious science", is science as it is conceived in the paradigm of complexity. In this context, organisations arise from a rigorous construction, reasoned from the collective project and applicable constraints. As distinct from the positivist and reductionist approach we mentioned earlier, this construction of an organisation is subject to critical deliberation. The organisation is a means to serve the collective, not an end to the benefit of a few.

are dissociated into separate disciplines according to their subject matter.

In the paradigm of complexity there emerges a complex of sciences, which can be distinguished but not separated. While there may be a boundary posited between sciences, its measure is not vanishing, it has a finite thickness.[38] We do not abruptly tip over from one to another, but transition through a *sfumato*, a *chiaroscuro*. And it is precisely in this neglected area where sciences are articulated together that we see those complex phenomena that conjoin several sciences.

At the heart of this new system of sciences, we find the sciences of mind (design science, cognitive science, neurophysiology, linguistics, philosophy, rhetoric, social anthropology, cognitive psychology, etc.)[39]

Around this core, there is a spiral of major scientific domains, organised in levels of emergence. They range from the physics of matter

---

38 The issues of the boundary layer in aerodynamics may be the hardest of that discipline, precisely because they deal with a boundary.

39 The fields of cognitive science, of complex systems, or of robotics, are examples of research fields which have arisen as multidisciplinary, being in fact organised around an object of study (the brain, thought processes, complex systems, robots) as opposed to a project. The development of these fields is hampered by the partitioning of universities into discipline-orientated sections. Indeed, institutions find it hard to identify researchers trained in such fields, and this is detrimental to their careers, while their contribution to knowledge is acknowledged to be essential.

and energy, in which biology and physiology take root, to information and organisation, and then anthropology, sociology and human sciences.

The human subject, who is a living being, is in turn the one capable of conception: it closes the loop of sciences, inasmuch as physical science, which it has designed, and which serves as the root of its self-conception, is itself a product with its anthropo-social conditioning.

Our project is to develop and disseminate a new concept of the system of sciences, which makes explicit their mutual articulations.

This presents major issues for the institutions where knowledge is constructed and transmitted. All major educational institutions are still based on a linear view, in which disciplines are separated by subject matter. As such they still fail to impart concepts adapted to the challenges of today's society. Institutions which would dare deploy this new vision would acquire a quality and relevance likely to be swiftly acknowledged in the field.

2.2 *Revisiting classical theories*

Classical theories receive a new illumination from the complex system of the sciences. Classical theories were defined by their subject matter. The associated scientific area, formed of theories and models, corresponds to the explanatory logic that is specific to that subject matter.

The fact that we are able to discern some discipline field (e.g., physiology) does not justify separating it from other fields. An object under study (e.g., adrenalin) in each classical theory (e.g., physiology) is articulated with, on the one hand, the level of emergence in which it is rooted (e.g., biology) and on the other with those for which it is a ground (e.g., psychology). It is possible to reconsider each classical theory in the light of this double articulation. No theory is isolated from others.

It is possible to review every theory in its systemic and organisational dimension. We can reformulate each theoretical problem within the semantics of the emergent paradigm, to shed new light on it, and to ask new questions.

This work to articulate and re-root the theories in the emerging paradigm is a meta-step, which enlarges the perspectives in each discipline. This work will reveal unknown dimensions and unmade conjunctions. Conversely, each discipline will be able to pursue new concrete investigations, following up on newly raised questions.

Welcome Complexity's project is to catalyse the work of scientists at the borders of their disciplines, to promote a new outlook on each discipline and to make possible a common way to look at them all.

There are major achievements at stake. Today we do not have the conceptual resources for thinking through our societies and organisations as systems where everything is connected. We think in a segmented manner, and this prevents us from acting on our societies as wholes. While we all are participants in society, in the degradation of the environment, in an unprecedented disparity of wealth, we are all powerless through lack of conceptual tools. As a result, some are still in a position to manipulate huge financial assets, with no sense of their responsibility to the rest of society. Elementary common sense is mocked, as we have no means to envision the collective dynamics which is our common outcome. Cumulated actions by everyone can precipitate the fall of the collective while no one can think it through and prevent it, and no one is able to clearly see their part of responsibility, which is evanescent in the systemic complexity and the emerging phenomena.

Enlightening the Community

1 Keeping watch and pointing out cases of oversimplification and degeneration

The classical paradigm is undermined by several types of degeneration:

- Degenerated knowledge development, reduced to operational manipulation,
- Live theorising reduced to a petrified doctrine, isolated and fenced in,
- Complex theory so shrunk that it fails to challenge our thinking.

Welcome Complexity's project includes a watch brief over such instances of degeneration. We feel that there is a civic duty to detect them, outline them and shed light on them in ways suitable for each population.

2 Applying an epistemology of new knowledge to enlighten ethics

The developing roots of the emerging paradigm enable the development of a theory of the Subject within the core of Science. It becomes possible to develop a critique of the Subject within, as well as thanks to, the epistemology associated to our new fields of knowledge.

Debating with philosophers, at the boundary of what we know, and know that we don't know, can shed light on ethics, without replacing it.

3 Developing critical thought among citizens

Ethical debate cannot be restricted to specialists. Civic governance and ethical deliberation require that every citizen is equipped with renewed modes of thought and action. In this project, it is essential to develop these capabilities for each stage of life, in a way that fits both the context (capability, location, history, belonging, etc.) and each person's specifics.

Welcome Complexity's project includes developing critical thought and discussion, an ability to design one's own modes of thought and action and skills for living and working together, for each generation.

4 Transitioning from humanism to humanances

4.1 *Origin and blind spots of humanism*

Entering a paradigm of complexity implies a transition in the way we conceive of human beings.

Humanism can be summarised as a philosophical and ideological position that emerged towards the end of the nineteenth century, as an *a posteriori* characterisation of the values and modes of thought of the "humanists", who originated the paradigm here labelled 'classical'. The ideology of humanism is marked by the intent to reposition human beings at the centre of things and to set up a value hierarchy where 'human values' predominate.

At its inception, the position of the humanists challenged the paradigm which was then dominant. They were struggling against a dogma of immutable, divine-given truth imposed on humans, and wanted to regain their autonomy and develop new directions. Struggling against scholasticism goes hand in hand with the scientific approach, which is the practical side of humanism. This approach is based on experiment. For a humanist, argument and refutation is based on fact, not on dogma. For the humanist, the task is to make use of reason to uncover universal natural law, without impediment from religious dogma.

As an ideology, humanism has blind spots. It carries a political and social project, implicit in 'classical' science, whose purpose is to discover natural law. This project is that of "order and progress". Such "enlightened" universalism was used as justification, outside western society, to obliterate the peculiarities of "unenlightened" people, who have been colonised, massacred or enslaved in the name of "order and progress". Within our own societies, this new faith in universal law has justified the programming of human beings[40].

Our societies have tended to be content with a conception of human beings inherited from the Enlightenment. We have tended to consider it as

---

[40] (1) To be sure, other periods of history have known erasing and programming of people seen as alien.

self-evident. Mere consciousness of one's existence, as available to each one of us, is nowhere near a real knowledge of oneself or of humanness. This lack of self-questioning is the symptom of selective blindness: the nature of knowing in a human being is probably what we know the least of.

4.2 *Humanances as emergence*

We can observe signs of struggle against the dominant ideology, the classical paradigm. This struggle endeavours to re-establish spaces of freedom, new directions, by rejecting 'blinkered thinking' when it loses its usefulness. We can see the rejection of classical political parties (whether left or right), the rejection of "the system", and many movements (Indignados, Podemos, Nuit Debout, Black Lives Matter, #metoo etc.), as relevant to this struggle (among other things). Such movements are still in search of a direction. We see them as aspirational: citizens wish for increased sovereignty in human societies which are increasingly complex.

The emerging paradigm is elaborating new directions in the conception of human beings, and of how we relate to ourselves, to others and to the world. It wants a more complex grasp, aligned with the multiplicity and the singularity of human persons and their relationships. We offer the term "humanances" for these new conceptions

We can sketch a new view of human beings as subjects: autonomous, interdependent, with some randomness and unpredictable elements of behaviour, interacting with the whole of the world of which they are part and in return are conditioned by.

This new view of human beings acknowledges the anthropo-socio-eco-technical complexity of our civilisation. It pushes us to reopen the political domain and redesign our living-together, with help from our new knowledge. It also offers an opportunity to consider the complexity of technological tools, which are both manipulable and manipulating, and mediate action both from us and on us.

Any conception of human beings entails a political project. Welcome Complexity's project has a political component, associated with an objective of living well and working well together. There is no party involved, just work on reshaping our view of human beings

Yet there is concrete stake in politics: we must provide conceptual instruments to generate a deep renewal of political thought and open new ways for our societies.

Conclusion: Institutionalising action

Along the way, we have envisioned a number of ways for action.

The intent is not to add to the individual and collective effervescence slowly and organically evolving in shadowy areas of the dominant paradigm, whether creating or reacting, whether conceptual or practical. All such elements are contributions to the emerging paradigm.

We are proposing to focus on the relationships among those elements, which are all too often isolated. The job is to be a coagulant for agents of transformation.

We think that the correct place to act is in co-building an institution that would catalyse:

- Developing new ways to deal with current problems,
- Developing an appropriate praxis,
- Joining again what has been disjoined,
- Constructing new scientific knowledge,
- Becoming aware of the network of 'humanances'.

Conclusion: To the action

What does Welcome Complexity do?

We work to ensure that each person is able to effect the changes seen as necessary to the development of their collective. In other words, we catalyse the dissemination and the mastery of the art and science of intelligently orchestrating each person's intelligence, from individuals through groups and organizations to the whole of society.

Welcome Complexity contributes to its ecosystem through the following lines of action (details in Appendix 4):

- **Observatory**: organising visibility and bridging between complexity research, leaders and practitioners;
- **Meeting place**: weaving productive links among each and every one, in a transdisciplinary, trans-sectorial, trans-functional, trans-cultural manner, imitating

the Macy conferences[41] and extending them to practitioners;

- **Apprenticeship and Companionship:** catalysing lifelong, multimodal learning of renewed ways of thinking and acting in complexity, using appropriate engineering, production and maintenance of the companionship process;
- **Network animation**: animating the community of learners, apprentices and companions: providing for knowledge and acknowledgement of the quality of learning and applying complexity as source and resource *in situ*;
- **Content**: making available and facilitating access to knowledge on essential collective processes, including in particular: clarifying stakes, examining a situation, reasoning, visualisation, deliberation, development of a shared vision, projecting into action, strategic planning, organization, transformation, etc.;
- **Research and Instrumentation (upstream)**: contributing to research on governance and organisation of collective action systems based on the emerging paradigm (2); contributing to the elaboration of new pathways and praxis; contributing to the development of relevant

---

[41] See e.g., 'Macy conferences' in Wikipedia

instrumentation for the activation of these new ways;

- Systemic, complex paradigm
- **Partnership projects in support of the associative ecosystem**: contributing to and supporting the learning of complexity in the rich emerging ecosystem, in synergy with intent and vocation;
- **Inductive[42] operational projects (downstream):** applying the art and science of thinking and acting in complexity *in situ*, by taking part in operational projects with high stakes or in operational projects designed to leverage learning situations.

When to contact *Welcome Complexity*?

We are a non-profit trusted third party, established on research, offering accompaniment.

We invite you to contact us when you begin to notice:

---

42 Operational projects are inductive because they exert a pull on learning. Learning the thinking and acting in complexity makes full sense only in a concrete situation, in which the learner tackles a project, an experiential situation. Learning is motivated by – and occurs in connection with – projects and situations which are felt as concrete.

- The need for renewed[43] modes of thought and action for the situations which you experience;
- The existence of renewed modes of *Thought and Action in Complexity*[44,45]
- The fact that these approaches are not simply a practice but form an art and a science;
- The fact that this art and this science combine into a praxis requiring epistemic, ethical and civic vigilance;

Our role is to provide any person lifelong accompaniment in life situations and in projects where they need to develop and apply this *Thought and action in complexity* which is of concern to all human beings, of any sociocultural character:[46] age (children, teenagers, adults,

---

43 In the realm of life, anything degenerates if it is not renewing itself. Traditional modes of thought and action, i.e., those rooted in the classical paradigm of positivist thought, tend to degenerate: they appear less and less capable of suitably guiding our action and our thought with regard to our perceived problems.

44 See Appendix 1 for a brief definition of complexity

45 In the face of growing inability of the traditional paradigm to provide intelligibility in the situations we experience, an emerging paradigm of COMPLEXITY has been developing – particularly over the past 70 years. This paradigm supports modes of thought and action which are better adapted for such situations.

46 While *Thought and action in complexity* is applicable regardless of sociocultural conditions, the design of learning resources, on the contrary, is closely dependent on them, as it must make the art and science accessible to each according to such characteristics.

seniors ...); function (workers, staff, management, executives, ...); job type (administration, collectives, education and research, health, industry, banking ...)

If you are facing a *complicated*[47] situation, you don't need us. A little time and money will suffice to discover a known, satisfactory solution.

If you are facing a *complex*[48] situation, there are no ready-made answers: it is necessary – with the contribution of the intelligence of all the stakeholders – to build an understanding, a vision, a strategy and a collective commitment. If you are in this kind of situation[49], it makes sense to contact us.

---

47 A complicated situation is not very different from a simple situation. In both cases the cluster of the problems is clearly predetermined. The question is how to resolve the problems, not to discover what it is. If the cluster is very large, especially if its size depends on the parameters of the problems, a resolution may be very complicated. Nonetheless it is purely a matter of algorithmic combinatorics.

48 A complex situation is one where the problem space is unknown: the problem needs to be discovered and formulated. This is of a completely different form than a complicated situation.

49 Here are a few clues that may, in the private sector, suggest the existence of a complex situation. Watch out for questions formulated in a reductionist or 'solutionist' way, e.g., in an environment which appears complex, uncertain, volatile, ambiguous, confused, how to improve our ways of working or living together? How to improve the management of projects, especially large ones? How to prioritize, and make enlightened decisions? How to identify opportunities? How to make meetings more dynamic? How to stand back and look at a situation? How to create a robust strategy? How to mobilize and involve the ecosystem of our partners and of citizens? How to make

This is what *Welcome Complexity* is all about, this is our offer to you.

Breaking out of isolation and connecting with *Welcome Complexity*

In a complex situation, you may very well manage by yourself; however:

Have you developed and matured the art and science of orchestrating the intelligences within your collective, in accordance with the context and in alignment with an objective?

In a complex situation, you may call on third parties specialized in providing reasoned answers to your questions; if so:

Do you maintain your independence from the thinking of these third parties? Do you rely on your collective, which experiences the problem and shall be required to tread the designed path? Are you confident that the 'solution concept' will take concrete flesh in the daily lives of your collective?

Do you trust the ethical and epistemological bases of these third parties? Can you be sure that they do not, consciously or not, bias the offered answers according to their own motivations?

---

others more autonomous? How to transform the culture of the collective? How to identify high potentials within the organization? How to secure support from a competent trusted third party to design and run my strategy?

Are you in a position to seek deep alternatives, reconnecting what was disjoined[50]? Are there no constraints arising from the segmentation of the offer along standard questions and answers inspired by traditional modes of thought and action[51]?

In a complex situation, you may call on expert facilitators. This may be appropriate, especially for point-wise intervention with human-sized groups; however:

Are these situations only experienced *point-wise*? To what extent do they extend to your daily functioning?

Do you have easy access to resources with the *personal ability and technical knowledge* to facilitate a group? Do you have access to enough of them, given the number of situations seen as complex in your collective?

Do you have easy access to resources able to *custom* design an intelligent orchestration of your collective? Do you have access to resources who

---

50 Such is the case, for instance, as to the conjunction and hybridisation, which most organizations still have to imagine, between human factors and technology, between vision and strategy, between strategy and organisation, between organisation and processes, between processes and job types, between job types and experience, between leaders and researchers. In general, the task is to launch regenerating conjunctions between competition logic and co-operation logic, between means and ends, between subjects and objects.

51 Consider this example of segmentation: on the one hand HR solutions, accompaniment, psychosocial risks; on the other, performance and productivity solutions, the LEAN approach.

have this ability for large multi-scale organizations?

Do you feel that such advanced technicians offering their services are keen to transfer these abilities to you? Do you feel that you are involved in an accompaniment that is intent on making you autonomous in these modes of thought and action?

Welcome Complexity is dedicated to developing the ability for personal and collective in the ecosystem. This requires catalysing this learning *in each person* and transferring to them the ability *to think and act in complexity*.

Appendix 1: What is Complexity?

A brief presentation of the concept

The world of phenomena overwhelms human faculties. When observing, or experimenting with, phenomena or systems, we may sometimes notice contradictions. Such contradictions always indicate some unknown or deep domain.

The concept of complexity refers to all such difficulties in grasping phenomena and systems marked by the conjunction of opposites such as order and disorder, whole and part, determinism and randomness, for which we never master all the relevant information. This missing information on phenomena we seek to understand is the most common situation.

We have all the relevant information only when we apply a reduction by means of thought patterns rooted in the classical paradigm: its approach to knowledge consists precisely in reducing phenomena to the point where our faculties are able to perceive and understand.

Is complex what is irreducibly woven together, and can be understood only by conjoining multiple components, which may sometimes seem contrary according to our usual logic. Complex exceeds our understanding. *Complex is the opposite of reducible.*

Any attempt to reduce a complex whole to a collection of disjoint parts destroys the intelligibility of the complex. The word *complexity* itself suggests this, by its associated word family: *plexus* = interlacing, *cum-plexus* = entanglement, connection, embracing, per-plexus=mixed-up, ambiguous, *multi-plexus* = multiplicity. The unity of what is woven together is the only warrant of its variety and intelligibility.

By definition, the complexity of a phenomenon or system cannot be simplified without losing its intelligibility. In the classical framework, we first disjoin phenomena then reduce them. A phenomenon is complex precisely because it forces us, in our quest for intelligibility, to unite notions which in the classical framework are separated and mutually exclusive.

A short bibliography

Complexity has a rich literature. Below is a drastically short list of references for anyone seeking an introduction:

1 Ashby, W. Ross, *An introduction to cybernetics.* New York: J. Wiley, 1956.

2 Atlan, Henri, *Entre le cristal et la fumée.* Paris: Seuil, 1986.

3 Bateson, Gregory, *Mind and Nature: A Necessary Unity.* Hampton Press, New edition, 2002.

4 Benkirane, Réda, *La complexité, vertiges et promesses.* Paris: Pommier, 2013.

5 Dumouchel, P., and Dupuy J.P., "L'auto-organisation, de la physique au politique." In *Colloque de Cerisy.* Paris: Seuil, 1994.

6 Genelot, Dominique, *Manager dans (et avec) la complexité: réflexions à l'usage des dirigeants.* Paris: Eyrolles, 2017.

7 Jullien, François, *The Silent Transformations.* Chicago: University of Chicago Press, 2011.

8 Kuhn, Thomas Samuel, *The Structure of Scientific Revolutions.* Chicago: University of Chicago Press, 1970.

9 Le Moigne, Jean Louis, *Le constructivisme - Tome 1 Les enracinements.* Paris: Harmattan Collection Ingenium, 2002.

10 Le Moigne, Jean Louis, and Morin Edgar. "Intelligence de la complexité : épistémologie et pragmatique." In *Colloque de Cerisy*. La Tour d'Aigues: Editions de l'Aube, 2005.

11 Montuori, Alfonso, *Complex Thought: An Overview of Edgar Morin's Intellectual Journey*. Metaintegral Foundation Resource Paper.

12 Morin, Edgar, *La Méthode - tome 3 La Connaissance de la connaissance*. Paris: Seuil, 2013.

13 Morin, Edgar, *Science avec conscience*. Paris: Poche, 1990.

14 Morin, Edgar, *Introduction à la pensée complexe*. Paris: ESF , 1990.

15 Morin, Edgar, *La méthode, tome 1. la nature de la nature*. Paris: Seuil, 1981.

16 Poteete, Amy R., and Marco A. Janssen, Elinor Ostrom. *Working together. Collective action, the commons, and multiple methods in practice*. New Jersey: Princeton University Press, 2010.

17 Ostrom, Elinor, *Governing the Commons: The Evolution of Institutions for Collective Action*. Cambridge, UK: Cambridge University Press, 1990.

18 Piaget, Jean, *Genetic Epistemology*. New York: Columbia University Press, 1970.

19 Prigogine, Ilya, and Isabelle Stengers, *La nouvelle alliance*. Paris: Gallimard, 1979.

20 Senge, Peter M., *The fifth discipline: the art and practice of the learning organization.* New York: Doubleday, 1990.

21 Simon, Herbert, *The Sciences of the Artificial.* Cambridge, MA: MIT Press, 2019.

22 Simon, Herbert, *Administrative Behavior: A Study of Decision-Making Processes in Administrative Organization.* New York: Macmillan Inc., 1947.

23 Simon, Herbert, *Models of Thought, Volume II.* New Haven, CT: Yale University Press, 1989.

24 Varela, Francisco, and Thomson, E., Rosch, E., *The Embodied Mind: Cognitive Science and Human Experience.* Cambridge, MA: MIT Press, 1991.

25 Von Foerster, Heinz, *Observing Systems: Selected Papers of Heinz Von Foerster,* Intersystems Publications, 1981.

26 Von Glasersfeld, Ernst, *Key Works in Radical Constructivism.* Intersystems Publications, 1981.

Research trends on complexity

Research streams concerning complexity can be subdivided as follows:

- In ***Third generation systemics*** – or complexity thought – complexity is seen as arising from the necessary multiplicity of viewpoints on any object. In this approach, a single viewpoint on some object or situation is generally partial and cripples the understanding. Therefore, it becomes indispensable to cross the outlooks and disciplines. Third generation systemics is the prime mover of the sciences of design.
- In ***Second generation systemics*** – or complex systems science – complexity is seen as arising from the characteristics of the objects under study. There are two sub-streams:
    - the study of the complexity of new types of mathematical objects. This touches on data-based design. In this perspective, the scientific domain of complexity relies on co-operation of mathematics and informatics and produces new objects at the boundary of these two domains.
    - the study of complexity as arising from the growth of the volume and origin of data. This touches on data-based perception. In this perspective, complex

systems research involves the development of new techniques supporting the creation of sense from abundant multi-scale data in many domains.

Types of organizations dealing with complexity

Action and thought in complexity touch all human organizations

- Multinationals, Large Enterprises
- Middle-sized, small and micro businesses
- Cooperatives & Mutuals
- NGOs, Associations, Societies...
- Local communities, Administrations
- Political parties, ...
- Independents, free-lances, individuals.

Emerging effervescence

Our society exhibits a growing effervescence. Below is a partial list of notable agencies in France which take part in this effervescence. We invite the reader to share with us effervescence in his/her country.

Agencies
Anvie
Ars Industrialis
ASHOKA (Association pour l'innovation citoyenne)
Association des cadres et dirigeants pour le progrès social et économique (ACADI)
Association française de systémique et de cybernétique (AFSCET)
Association Française pour l'Ingénierie des Système (AFIS)
Association sur évolution de la conscience
Association Teilhard de Chardin
ATD quart monde
ATTAC, association des sociétés coopératives
Barbare the family
Bateson Symposium
Bleu, Blanc, Zèbre
Boson projects
Centre culturel international de Cerisy
Centre de Recherche Interdisciplinaire (CRI)
Centre edgar morin à l'EHESS
Centre français de sociocratie, le Centre mondial de sociocratie (CMS)
Centre Michel Serre
CESAMES: architecture des systèmes

Changer d'ère
Club de Budapest
Colibris
Collectif Roosevelt
Collège des Bernardins
CRG centre de recherche en gestion
CSO - Centre sociologie des organisations
CTEL centre transdisciplinaire d'épistémologie et des arts vivants
CVT Athena
Débat
Devoxx
Dialogues en Humanité
Edition Leopold Meyer
Engage
Entreprise et progrès
Esprit
Essec chaire de la complexité
Faber Novel
Fondation maison des sciences de l'homme
Fondation pour les progrès de l'homme FPH
Fondation Science Citoyenne
Futurible
Idées d'Après
Ingénieur Sans Frontière (IESF)
Institut de recherche et débat sur la gouvernance (IRG).
Institut de Recherche sur l'Innovation (IRI)
Institut de recherche technologique « numérique des systèmes du futur
Institut des Hautes Etudes pour la Science et la Technologie (IHEST)
Institut IFEAS - systémiques appliquées
Institut National des Systèmes Complexes

Institut protestant de théologie Ricoeur association
L'institut de l'entreprise
Le cercle des économistes
Le mouvement des makers
Le mouvement open source
Le Réseau National des Systèmes Complexes (RNSC)
L'École de Paris du management
Les économistes atterrés
Les initiatives citoyennes
MCX-APX intelligence de la complexité
MOM 21
Mouvement Colibris
Mouvement du convivialisme
Nous Citoyens
OuiShare
Philolab
Prospective 2100
Réseau National des Systèmes Complexes (RNSC)
Revue Thérapie Familiale
Society for Organizational Learning (SOL)
Synlab
Terre de Conscience
Theconversation.com
Trust management institute
Vision 2021
World Organisation of Systems and Cybernetics (WOSC OMSC) International Federation for Systems Research (IFSR) Union Européenne de Systémique (UES-EUS)
X-Sciences de l'Homme et de la Société
X-Sursaut

Appendix 2: Concrete examples of complexity

A branching of methodological components from a common, unacknowledged stem

Many methods and trends in management exist, with distinct intents and contexts of relevance, yet with common roots which are often unnoticed.

Approach	Brief presentation
Agile Software Development	This is a method for development of software applications which focuses on the process of creation, anticipating the required flexibility and taking a pragmatic approach to the finished product. Agile Software Development is centred on maintaining simple, well-documented code, with frequent testing and immediate delivery of components as they become ready. The principle is to rely on small increments accepted stepwise by the client, as opposed to a single delivery of a large application at the end of the project.
Scrum	The SCRUM method proposes a framework for the realization of complex projects. Initially designed for software projects, this method is quite simply applicable to any type of project.
Devops	Devops is a movement to align all teams of the information system on a common objective, starting with DEV teams in charge of the evolution of the system and extending to the OPS teams who have responsibility for infrastructure (operators, system managers, network, databases, etc.)
Design thinking	This is an approach to innovation seeking to synthesize analytical and intuitive thought. It relies on a co-creation process with feedback from the intended user.
Systems engineering	Systems engineering is an interdisciplinary scientific approach intended to formalise and successfully master the design of complex systems.

Approach	Brief presentation
Enterprise architecture	Enterprise architecture involves cross-analysis of horizontal components (domains of the enterprise, such as business lines, support) and vertical components (architectural layers, such as business processes, applications, infrastructure) with the aim of removing partitions and discovering cross-synergies, for a better management of complexity. EA aims at supporting change in the enterprise, controlling impacts. It assists the enterprise in building capability and firming up interdependencies.
Design Science	Design Science studies the processes of design
Collective intelligence	The term COLLECTIVE INTELLIGENCE refers to the cognitive abilities of a community which arise from multiple interactions among its members (agents). The knowledge of individual members is restricted to a partial awareness of the environment, and they are not conscious of all the elements which influence the group.
Digital	The term DIGITAL is in widespread use for a large number of daily practices which we do not clearly understand, and which have a profound effect beyond mere technology.
Maieutic strategy	This term is used in philosophy to refer to the investigation of knowledge. Socrates, whose mother was a midwife, talked of "assisting minds to give birth". In this process of concrete, pseudo-naive questioning, Socrates used to listen and arrange for his interlocutor to become aware of imprecision or contradiction in reasoning. Thus, a person could come to realize that they did not really know what they thought they knew. Conversely, they could be led to become aware of things they actually knew.

Approach	Brief presentation
Nonviolent communication	This is a language developed by Marshall B. Rosenberg. According to the author, it is "the language and interaction which reinforce our ability to benevolent giving and inspiring others with the wish to do the same". Empathy is central to this communication process launched in the seventies, in common with Carl Rogers' person-centred therapy. (Rosenberg was a student of Rogers). The term nonviolent refers to Gandhi's movement: it means communicating harmlessly with another.
Co-development	Professional Co-development is a learning approach that relies on the group and on the interactions between the participants to support the achievement of the fundamental objective: improving professional practice. The thinking is supported by structured exercises in consulting about issues actually faced by the participants.
Mediation	Mediation is a discipline or practice which defines the intervention of a third party to facilitate the exchange of information, or to clarify or establish relationships. The third party, called MEDIATOR, is neutral, independent and impartial. The activity varies according to context; however, any third-party intervention presents constant features, including elements of pedagogy and relationship quality.

Approach	Brief presentation
Appreciative Inquiry	Appreciative Inquiry is a method of change management which appeared at the end of the 1980's at Case Western Reserve University. It was developed by Pr. David Cooperrider and his associates. The first premise of Appreciative Inquiry is that every enterprise has some aspect which works well, source of its vitality, effectiveness and success. Appreciative Inquiry starts with discovering what is positive and already works within the scope of the assignment and of the team's objectives. This POSITIVE CORE is used as a fulcrum to energize and inspire new projects.
Organizational Coaching	Organizational Coaching is the coaching of a human system composed of teams (or teams of teams). As in any form of coaching, the purpose is to support the system toward intended results, as different from the current situation. The intended changes can be any of: Restructuring, mergers, acquisitions; Reorganisations, ERP changes; Strategic reorientations, breakthroughs; Enterprise culture transformation
Team coaching	Team coaching is a specific practice. It is complex in that it must address both the individual persons and the whole of the group.
Facilitation	Group facilitation is a process chosen and accepted by all members of the group. Facilitators, sufficiently neutral and without decision power, inquire and facilitate in order to assist the group in identifying and resolving problems, making decisions and improving group effectiveness.

Approach	Brief presentation
Labs	This term refers to an arrangement enabling multiple agents to create many innovations which can be easily tested by users. A lab facilitates the design of products, services or technologies, or also socially useful inventions. It facilitates the study of user and consumer behaviours and the discovery of solutions that will promote behavioural change. From this work comes the discovery of new markets. A lab is open and flexible and promotes participation. It supports the development of ideas, thoughts and concepts by providing the necessary tools to apply them. It is a reliable and attractive mode of reflection. The term appears in a variety of expressions and is used for various purposes.
Living labs	A living lab is a user-centred, open-innovation ecosystem for experimentation and co-creation.
Fab labs	A fabrication laboratory is a 'third-space', kind of makerspace, devised by the Massachusetts Institute of Technology (MIT) and the FabFoundation; it offers a minimal inventory to support the establishment of 'fablab projects', a set of open-source or free software called Fab Modules and a governance charter, the Fab Charter.

Approach	Brief presentation
Social Lab	A social lab focuses on practical innovations to address complex social challenges; they present three characteristic features: Social labs involve many contributors, including concerned parties, whereas a planning approach would rely on a small group of experts to develop a high-end solution, with command and control. Social labs are experimental, using trial and error to manage a portfolio guiding investment decisions, as opposed to a planning approach which would put all eggs in a single basket. Social labs adopt a system-based approach, addressing the challenges at root-cause level, whereas a planning approach might address symptoms instead of the causes of a social problem
Palo Alto school	The Palo Alto school is a line of thought and research named after the city of Palo Alto, California, starting in the 1950's. References to this school appear in psychology, psychosociology and the sciences of information and communication in relation to cybernetic concepts. Among other things, this school originated family therapy and brief therapy. It was founded by Gregory Bateson with contributions from Donald D. Jackson, John Weakland, Jay Haley, Richard Fisch, William Fry and Paul Watzlawick. The key points of the approach are to consider that the understanding of symptoms comes from understanding the interactions between people and the constraints of the environment and not from the collection of individuals taken in isolation.

Approach	Brief presentation
Systemic family therapy	This is a specific psychotherapeutic technique aimed at facilitating exchanges among members of a family. The theoretical bases of family therapies are linked to two currents of thought called First-order and Second-order cybernetics, arising from "System theory". Hence the name systemic and communication family therapy They were first developed in California in the 1950's, and have then been enriched by observations and reflection in European schools in the 1980's
Neurolinguistic Programming	In psychology, Neurolinguistic Programming (NLP) is a method for acting on behaviour by means of language. More precisely, it is "a psychotherapeutic practice and model originating in the formalizing of communicative and clinical practices of some exceptional therapists": NLP attempts to model successful strategies of acknowledged experts and transmit them to others.
Dynamic spiral	During the development of an individual, an organization or a society, new models of the world appear, superimposed on older ones in an endless evolutionary spiral. Such paradigms are known as memes. Even though they assist in managing an increasingly complex world, no meme is better than another. A level of existence is appropriate inasmuch as it is adequate to our living conditions.

Approach	Brief presentation
Community management	Community Management (CM) consists in animating and federating communities on the Internet in the service of a company, a brand a celebrity or an institution. This specialism, closely linked with Web 2.0 and the development of social networks, is still evolving. At its core are the interaction and exchanges with internauts (animation, moderation); however, the community manager can take up various activities depending on context.
Sociocracy	Sociocracy is a mode of governance enabling an organization of any size – family to country – to operate efficiently without any centralised power structure, using a self-organizing mode with distributed decision-making. Its current mode arose in 1970 from systemic theory. Sociocracy relies on the freedom and co-responsibility of participants. Within a logical frame of self-organization trusting human nature, it harnesses the power of collective intelligence to serve the achievement of common objectives. It therefore makes it possible to reach a common objective together, while respecting persons and preserving the diversity of viewpoints and contributions, on the basis of quality interpersonal relationships. As opposed to more recent developments such as Holacracy, the sociocratic model is open and royalty-free. Sociocracy makes original use of certain democratic techniques such as candidateless election and decision by consent. The difference between sociocracy and democracy is that democracy applies to a group of persons which may have no relationship, whereas sociocracy involves persons engaged in an organization and thereby maintaining more proximate connections.

Approach	Brief presentation
Holacracy	Holacracy is a system for organizing governance based on the formalised leveraging of collective intelligence. In operation it makes it possible to distribute the decision mechanisms through a fractal organization of self-organizing teams. This clearly distinguishes it from top-down, pyramidal models. Holacracy has been adopted by several organizations – USA, France, UK, Germany, New Zealand. While often compared with sociocracy, it is significantly different from it.
Organizational learning	Organizational learning is the process of creation, maintenance and transmission of knowledge within an organization. An organization progressively improves through experience. Out of experience it can extract widespread knowledge, covering any topic liable to improve the organization. As examples, there could be means to increase effectiveness in production, or ways to develop beneficial relationships with investors. Knowledge can be created in four categories: individual, collective, organizational and interorganizational.
Organization Development	Organization Development is an effort planned at organization level and led by Management to improve the effectiveness and health of the organization. It takes the form of interventions in organizational processes making use of behavioural science. Tools for organizational development contribute to aligning strategy, structure, management processes, HR processes as well as performance measurement and rewards.

Illustration through the Uber case in France

1 The Uber case is a concrete example of a problem situation which cannot be resolved by classical means

France was faced with an unexpected crisis in the sector of taxis, with the swift entry of a disruptive actor, Uber.

The State is lagging behind in two ways:

- It retreats behind the old rules which used to make sense but have become obsolete,
- It did not anticipate and propose a thorough reform, in which it could have taken a powerful position as regulator of the private vehicle transport ecosystem; such reform could have been organized around a business platform controlled by the French or European powers.

It would have been possible to foresee the entry of Uber and to view it in the light of an understanding of the current mutation. Faced with the challenge, France was not able to find a satisfactory solution: stakeholders are in conflict and freeze their positions, unable to step back sufficiently to find new pathways.

2 How could this situation have been avoided?

The old way consists in establishing a group of experts and delegate the search for a solution to them. The Attali report, which is brilliant, contained a set of proposals on the question of Paris taxis. It was not followed through for political reasons: because certain parties have not been involved in the solution, the report is subject to conflict.

Given the new ways of thought and action, the person in charge would engage, not some expert but the collective of those persons concerned directly, in order for them to build a pathway that they find satisfactory. The person in charge must be prepared to delegate and to trust, not knowing ahead of time the nature of the outcome.

These new approaches provide a possibility to design in a conscious and ethical manner a *process* that will bring about a resolution of the problem, emerging from the collective concerned.

The work will be based directly on the business experience of persons who are directly involved in the problem. There is no expert from outside, no advisors carrying out interviews and proposing brilliant reports. There is a collective working by consensus on the need to elaborate together a pathway that is satisfactory for everyone, in the respect of each other.

The design of the process requires working on the way in which the collective will research and document the problem. The point is not to find a solution from outside, but to bring about a resolution through an organic process. The task is to design the process whereby the collective will bring forth a path for resolution; this process being judged satisfactory in the intersubjective consensus. This work requires, upstream, an epistemic awareness of processes whereby knowledge emerges within a collective, and, downstream, appropriate ethics in the facilitator supporting the collective while respecting the process as designed.

3 Some aspects of the design process

Without prejudging the outcome, we can observe common features in all emerging practices: it will be the task of the proposed institution to provide an adequate formulation.

A typical process makes use of sessions engaging the stakeholders of the problem. These sessions are highly structured and facilitated by a benevolent third party, from outside the problem, who facilitates the co-construction in a flexible but firm manner. This third party does not serve any person but serves the goal of the collective. This is a new and subtle specialism of *complex facilitation*. The facilitator guarantees:

- The rigor of the steps followed by the collective to elucidate the problem and formulate new knowledge (*epistemic guarantee*),
- The quality of the deliberative work among stakeholders (*ethical guarantee*).

The process makes possible a dynamic adaptation of the way in which stakeholders conceive of the system object they share (e.g., the system of private vehicle transportation). It uses simple concrete, systematic questions:

- *what is the objective?*
- *what is its use?*
- *why is there such a need today?*
- *is this a long-term function?*
- *etc.*

The systematic nature of the questioning guarantees that:

- the approach creates a ratchet effect,
- the advance is controlled,
- the process terminates,
- the results are robust and known to be appropriate.

In our example, the stages of the process might include the following objectives:

- Specifying viewpoints and dimensions to take into account: users, driver, taxes, security, ...
- Choosing the participants for the working collective on the basis of their proven competence in connection with the problem and of their ethical leadership as acknowledged by their peers,
- Establishing the working collective on human and interpersonal relationship among stakeholders. This stage often is the

most delicate. It is necessary to ensure that stakeholders shall not be mere role players,

- Co-establishing ethical rules for the following discussion, to ensure that they will be shared,
- Launching a critical deliberation to bring about an explicit, complete and shared understanding of the problem situation as perceived,
- Making explicit satisfactory pathways from this new understanding;

Such a highly structured, sustained questioning by the animator quickly produces value for the collective. It brings about:

- A calming of conflicts and tensions among stakeholders,
- A shared description of the problem situation,
- An identification of more or less severe divergences among intents, interests and concepts of stakeholders,
- An identification of stakeholders' blind or shadow zones,
- The imagining and devising of new pathways.

As the exchanges progress, each person steps out of their initial position and begins to understand that of others. A shared, richer conception develops, covering all viewpoints, and not limited by the abilities of an expert.

4 The benefits of elucidation work

There would have been several benefits to the work of elucidating the problem arising from new technologies in the economic and business models in the taxi sector:

- Such work would have prepared the ground for new initiatives by French startups: Uber could have been French,
- It would have shed light on social, political and legal issues, and facilitated any necessary evolution. Among other things, it would very early have distinguished *on-demand* platforms, where the intermediary monopolises the exchange value, from collaborative *commonwealth* platforms, where value is distributed as *fair share* according to each actor's contributions.

The whole exercise would have highlighted a new role for the State. In such a context, the role of the State takes on many characteristics of the kinds of praxis currently emerging. For instance, the State would simultaneously have to:

- Take a step back, with no direct intervention, instead of its current logic of regulation by legislation,
- Especially not yield to *laissez-faire*. On the contrary the State would more than ever play a role of trustee, establishing and dynamically maintaining the rules of the

game among actors, with a civic finality instead of a purely financial one.

5 How does this differ from an expert panel?

The work of elucidation is not a complement of classical approaches, nor is it opposed to them. It is not *another approach to social management*[52]. It is a meta-approach which revisits the epistemological roots of approaches, i.e., the process whereby a human collective develops a form of knowledge.

This difference from an expert panel approach arises from the fact that a facilitated elucidation by the collective:

- Produces an outcome that cannot be predicted, nor manipulated,
- Ensures a confrontation with experiential reality, thus eliminating any pathways that would ignore the constraints of reality,
- Produces knowledge that is closely adapted to the context,
- Avoids the pitfalls of abstract logical thought,
- May end up with a pathway that is very similar or very different to what an expert panel might have produced,

---

52 Often heard, this kind of off-the-cuff dismissal misses the essential purpose of complex facilitation.

- Can be accomplished without any recourse to external expertise (except possibly for point-wise contributions).

Elucidation work is never conclusive: it does not produce a solution, but a temporary untangling. It must be resumed as soon as constraints, context or objectives are perceived to have evolved significantly. It is a collective praxis that enables the collective to maintain consistency and meaning in its collective action system.

The very features of the elucidation approach ensure that:

- The objective is never sought without the involvement of persons who are directly concerned with the problem,
- Concerned actors are structurally committed to the project as defined,
- Necessary viewpoints are understood mutually by all stakeholders,
- Actors acquire a better representation not only of themselves, but also of the meaning and place of their action in the collective,
- The project integrates all necessary viewpoints,
- The quality of the cognitive processing, as facilitated by the third party, relies on an understanding of the way in which knowledge is developed,
- The pathways produced closely fit the specifics of the context,

- The sponsor of the work can securely delegate the investigation of a problem for which they have responsibility and which they have not succeeded in resolving satisfactorily.

Some comments on previous concrete achievements

The principals of the current project have had many opportunities to deploy these new modes of thought and action, at all levels of organizations. The context of the client has often allowed only for a partial application, sometimes without explicit sponsorship. There was a notable exception: these modes were deployed globally in a concrete case involving a group of 150 persons (budget of the direction: EUR 40M) within a large organization (EUR 700M budget)

According to the leader of the group: "*This approach produced excellent results. I have personally been surprised by their quality. I was not a believer at the start. In addition to the direct deliverables of the working groups – target processes, best practices and resolution of dysfunction – I noted a significant improvement of internal cross-dialog and smoother work relationships among agents. There has also been a significant enhancement in understanding the nature of the organization and its global objectives, in the motivation of each person to take part and in the role each is assuming in the achievement of these objectives...*"

Here are some direct quotes from the participants in the exercise:

"This was quality, important work"

"Impressive: it seems so far back (the initial state of affairs), and yet it is not. A year ago, it was a shambles, now we have 3 meetings, in a sober mode."

"It's not just talk, there something concrete there"

"It was an opportunity to stand back"

"It was a rich opportunity, a group of people of the same job type, where we can share and exchange to make progress together, in a fixed, structured slot"

"At the beginning there were more problems than now; we did not know if it was just us, or everybody. It's reassuring to realize we all have the same problems"

The same participants give the following comments on the approach:

"In 2009 you had to drag us there; later, it became like ... a drug ... (laughter)"

"It is important that these meetings were compulsory. Otherwise we would always have something else to do"

"To be fruitful, collective work must be institutionalized as meetings; even an individual genius by himself, that does not work. To institutionalize requires a lot of effort, and appropriate resources, or else it will fail. We have known that in the past, micro-actions left and right; they tell us 'go ahead, make a proposal'; you write n documents, n gizmos, n feedbacks and it

ends up against a wall. We need collective work, and well-known resources, to succeed in making a change in consensus"

"The hierarchy may accept our recommendations if it fits in the cycle of the approach; if it comes directly from us, I am not sure it would be accepted. We need this certification."

"We must find the right rhythm, the proper time to convey the recommendations we have reached by consensus"

"We (operational staff) have done the walking, but you (facilitators) have been holding our hand."

An essential point: the project principals have from the start maintained a pragmatic approach. Only later, observing the power of the process, have they sought a conceptual backing for their work, by researching the existing body of knowledge. In this search, they discovered:

1. That these modes of thought and action are deeply rooted in a set of emerging research trends,
2. That there are a number of practices arising, which are analogous though different in detail.

Appendix 3: Primers for Thoughtful Practitioners

Welcome Complexity's project is to support scrutiny of problem situations, to regenerate the way we think of them and open perspectives on action. A question naturally arises: what are the topics that deserve priority and concrete work within this project? Investigating this issue is a first step to be undertaken with the collective of thoughtful practitioners. Let's try a few primers here.

1 Thinking through the World system

For the first time in humanity's history, a world system exists within which we are strongly interdependent. We do not yet master concepts to think this system through, as an organised whole in which we all take part. This being the case, how could we design appropriate organisation and governance to deal with the challenges facing us? How can we think how each relates to us all? How can each assume their responsibility in the system?

2 Thinking through human responsibility, autonomy and sovereignty

A constant of human experience is a relationship to some supreme authority, whether nature, some deity or some universal law. How can we encourage each one not to fob off their personal responsibility on the supreme authority? How can we assume our responsibility, our sovereignty, our autonomy in the face of the existential anguish of radical uncertainty and full responsibility? How can we develop our responsibility in freedom, not on the fear of some authority that must be placated?

3 Thinking through the conjoining of scientific disciplines

By way of an example, consider the difficult linkage between biology and psychology. Developmental psychology generally agrees that in the absence of language and attention from its surroundings, a child fails to thrive. Understanding the psychological layer depends essentially on understanding the relationship to the environment. On the other hand, biology generally agrees that a cell's functioning can be understood essentially on the basis of internal principles and mechanisms, and that its environment is merely a reserve of resources. Apparently these two modes of thinking are antagonistic. And yet a human being has both a biological and a psychological nature. Tough problem.

4 Thinking through the design processes

Processes of design are still hampered by a lack of recognition and integration: split between technology and anthropo-socio-ecology; split between system architecture, project management, system engineering; split between complex system science and design science...

We have within our reach a deep and consistent connection among the approaches of psychology, neurology, cognitive science, social science, informatics and physical science. At stake in this conjoining work is a great leap forward, an opening of our insight into the way we produce our knowledge, our techniques and our artefacts (vehicles, devices, robots, etc.). At stake is the establishing of new, renewed, consistent foundations for rational human thought, including theoretical physics.

Appendix 4: *Welcome Complexity:* from intention to action

In this Manifesto we have established the roots of *what for* and *why*.

This establishing stance is appropriate. But it says nothing about actions which shall embody this vision. The root locus of *Welcome Complexity* is a project, to be embodied and realized as concrete interactions with its ecosystem.[53] The questions then arising are "OK, but *what?* and *how?*". Such questions are particularly justified as they are asked by our patrons, who want to know the concrete value of their proposed support for *Welcome Complexity*.

Every interaction of *Welcome Complexity* with persons in its environment is intended to spread renewed and rooted ways of acting and thinking in complexity, to instil the epistemic and

[53] This ecosystem is composed of all forms of organisation, as outlined in Appendices 1 & 2.

ethical roots of the praxis, to bring about conditions which favour their acquisition and, by exercising this praxis, to stimulate the emergence of alternatives in facing those problems that the collective currently considers intractable.

Welcome Complexity shall have outlived its usefulness when all collectives have developed:

- each person's autonomous capability of acting and thinking in complexity;
- the collective's autonomous capability of strategic governance and continuous adaptation to its environment;
- an epistemic and ethical imperative which each person perceives as a necessary condition for development and maintenance of those capabilities, not as an external constraint.

Uniqueness of the *Welcome Complexity* project

The special uniqueness of this project is its construction, which resists yesterday's modes of action, and instead, by its very constitution, offers to experiment with tomorrow's ways of action and conception.

The envisioned institution is a locus where complementary viewpoints – which usually eschew confrontation and dialogue – are joined, never dissociated: research and practice, old and new generations, 'classical' and emerging modes of thought and action, co-design and co-realization, object and subject, 'geeks' and 'luddites'[54] who resist technology.

The project is thus unique, not so much in its intent as in its mode of progression, between two conjoined poles that make its strength:

- **A transition of epistemological paradigm** which is in progress within research itself and is slowly outlining the unity behind the diversity of the effervescence: at this depth are being elaborated those principles which underlie all new modes of acting and thinking in

54 A geek is a person who has an intense passion for some domain. The term is often used in connection with 'cultures of imagination' (genre cinema, comic books, video games, role play, etc.) or with science, technology or IT. A luddite was a member of gangs of English textile workers who, led by Ned Ludd (1811-13 & 1816) were intent on destroying the new weaving machines which they held responsible for unemployment.

complexity. The paradigm of complexity[55] is very fruitful: it renews the insight and the ability to open up new outlooks on problems raised by the current transition. It makes it possible to design new approaches adapted to the specific issues of each organisation (business, scale, ...)[56] Such new modes of production are radically more efficient,[57] but require from the collective a profound cultural transition.[58]

---

[55] The paradigm of complexity develops in parallel with the growth of emergent sciences, among which: cognitive science, systems engineering, sciences of complexity, design science.

56 The design of new, emerging economic models (called functional, collaborative and circular) makes massive borrowings – most often unaware – from new modes of design belonging in the paradigm of complexity (function of a system in its environment, interactions among components and with the environment, feedback from the environment). There is a deep conjunction: the key notions underlying the socioeconomic transition are those of the epistemological transition from positivism to constructivism, corresponding to the transition from the matter-energy layer to the information-organisation layer. For instance, behind socioeconomic systems of partnerships within the digital economy, we find a notion developed in the science of complexity: that of structural coupling of mutual advantages and disadvantages. We also find the semantics of transition: from linear quantity to circular quality, from chain to ecosystem, etc.

57 The efficiency of the new models arises from them drawing, among other things, on multiscale logics, on the autonomy and creativity of human beings, on structural coupling between systems, on the dynamics of synergy and antagonism, co-operation and competition, and on tooling designed to be handy, amplifying human action rather that replacing it.

[58] Profound cultural transition for the collective: the anthropological challenge is to facilitate the transition from a culture based on a program dictated from the top and cascading down to one of autonomy

- **The exercising in context of a new praxis**, which we call *complex facilitation* for lack of a better term. In this emerging praxis the focus is on examination rather than analysis, conjunction before separation, search for the possible rather than the necessary, proscriptive rather than prescriptive stance, regularities and constraints rather than laws. This praxis is suitable for the construction of new pathways: it tends to re-establish watchfulness as to the limits of expertise, as to randomness, as to the role of emotions and intuition in mental work.

This fundamental *praxis/ epistemology* dipole induces many singularities as follows:

- take account of the dimensions of action (business action), of context (systemics, architecture) and of human nature,
- propose an inductive approach based on daily reality: (theory/model of *what works* rather than application of generic principles),
- exploit a lode of interdisciplinary skills often ignored in organisations,
- Leverage the latest developments in Science and Technology,

---

(and *ingenium*) at each scale level. The *leader* becomes a *pilot*. The *operator* becomes a *responsible agent*.

- Break up discipline silos to better serve the unknotting of complex problems,
- Acknowledge the human dimension (cognitive, psychological, physiological) implicated in processes of change in organisations and human systems,
- Acknowledge the dimension of emergences in human collectives, in particular the meta-design of human systems (rules and principles of self-organisation in support of a given finality),
- Acknowledge the social dimension: anthropology, sociopsychology,
- Catalyse the creation of new pathways for organisations.

The nature of the project will naturally bring it closer to the various emerging organisations, each with remarkable accomplishments,

However, all those institutions have a common tropism, associated with yesterday's world from which they have arisen. Each of these institutions practices one or more of the following dissociations:

- Between knowledge and life experience: most often relying on breakfast meetings and task forces, and publishing reports and expert conclusions. There is no cycling between life experience – the concrete experience of managers *in situ* – and a stepping back from which a valid, transmissible knowledge can arise,

- Between research/teaching and enterprise: typically, research produces knowledge, managers listen. Or, managers speak, but research does not follow up on this life experience to produce knowledge. There is no *co-construction* of knowledge from life situations,
- Between innovating start-ups and established enterprises: these two cultures are generally dissociated. While enterprises, the heart of today's economy and employment, are most centrally concerned in the mutation, they have no connection with the start-ups, which have the desirable cultural orientation.

Welcome Complexity's Work tracks

Welcome Complexity's contributions to the ecosystem (business, administration, local communities, associations, NGO's, individuals,...)	**Work tracks**
Observatoire *Bridge-building among complexity research, leaders and practitioners (researchers in complexity sciences, psychologists, ethnologists, cognitive scientists, neuroscientists, neurosurgeons, epistemologists, philosophers, artists, leaders, managers, practitioners, consultants, coaches, facilitators, etc.)*	Interviewing persons eminent in the field of complexity, Surveys, questionnaires and interviews among leaders and practitioners facing complex situations in the field, The Observatory of Complexity, Environmental intelligence, Reading notes and Bibliography of Complexity science, Integration of research.
Meeting Venue *Weaving productive links for all and sundry*	Meetings for dedicated small groups (workshops, breakfasts, etc.), Learning trips, Dedicated seminars, Conferences, General publications, Identifying and specifying questions and problems as perceived.
Apprenticeship and Companionship *Catalysing lifelong learning on regenerated modes of thought and*	Andragogical engineering and production Experimenting and discovering instruments,

Welcome Complexity's contributions to the ecosystem (business, administration, local communities, associations, NGO's, individuals,...)	**Work tracks**
action in complexity	Micro-learning seminars, Learning workshops
Network animation *Facilitating the community of learners,* *Introducing and recognising apprentices and companions in complexity*	Animation Platform for continuous exchange Co-optation Diffusion
Contents *Facilitating access to knowledge and practice of key processes (joined representation, modelling, reasoning, deliberation, organisation, governance)* *Scrutinising the challenges, examining situations, visualising, purposeful description, purposeful contextualisation, reasoning on models, simulating and interpreting, deliberating, governing, forecasting, organising, transforming)*	Conceptual foundations, Reporting on experience Providing notes, kits and practical manuals for groups Book of Knowledge (BOK)

Lignes de produit	Produits
Research and instrumentation (upstream) *Contributing to research on governance and organisation of collective action systems,* *Contributing to the development of new paths and praxes,* *Contributing to the development of relevant instrumentation for the activation of these new paths.*	Chair and other positions Instrumentation Publishing
Projects in partnership in support of the associative ecosystem *Contributing to, and supporting learning of complexity in the emerging rich ecosystem*	Co-development and support
Operational projects (downstream) *Practicing the art and science of thought and action in complexity, in situ: learning is motivated by -- and achieved within – projects and situations which are apprehended as concrete problems.* *Contributing to creating conditions which promote the emergence of alternatives to current models.*	'Real' case studies Investigation with adequate tools Bespoke facilitation for *ad hoc* support Bespoke in-depth support Vision and deep transformation of the trade, suitable for a transition in the active paradigm (so-called 'digital')

Founding Members of *Welcome Complexity*

Name	**Brief career notes**	**Role in *Welcome Complexity***
Michel PAILLET	President of *X-Sciences de l'Homme et de la Société*, Honorary president of *XMP-Consult* (an association of consultants from major engineering schools), consultant, coach and facilitator. Engineer, Harvard Visiting Fellow, PhD in economics, joint perspective of economy and psycho-socio-anthropology.	President
Jean-Pierre DANDRIEUX	Expert on organisational transformation, as afforded by IT and new technologies, PhD in informatics and algorithmics (issues of constraint resolution). https://www.linkedin.com/in/jdandrieux/?originalSubdomain=fr	Vice-President
Jérome LAZARD	Co-founder and executive of *Idéoscripto*, a specialist firm in design and animation of executive seminars and of workshops for change awareness. https://www.linkedin.com/in/j%C3%A9r%C3%B4me-lazard-2794a620/?originalSubdomain=fr	Secretary
Jérémie AVEROUS	Founder of *Project Value Delivery*, a consulting firm specialised in management of large complex projects (€500 million to €1.5 billion) www.projectvaluedelivery.com	Treasurer

Name	Brief career notes	Role in *Welcome Complexity*
Philippe FLEURANCE	Former athlete, researcher and former director of the Laboratory for Sport psychology and ergonomy, vice-president of *Intelligence de la complexity (MCX)* https://www.linkedin.com/in/philippefleurance/?originalSubdomain=fr	Board Member
Dominique GENELOT	Former executive of consulting firm *INSEP Consulting*, author	Board Member
Pascale RIBON	Executive involved in fostering innovation & deeptech for the French government TEDx Saclay: https://www.youtube.com/watch?v=6fmWo-znXVM	Board Member
Laurent DANIEL	President of a Think tank, Senior economist at OECD in charge of industry http://www.x-sursaut.org/	Board Member
Dominique LUZEAUX	Doctor (HDR), working in the French Ministère de la Défense on expertise and management of projects and complex systems engineering for the armed forces Former president of the french chapter of the international Council on System Engineering *INCOSE* https://www.incose.org/	Board Member

Name	Brief career notes	Role in *Welcome Complexity*
Philippe VAN DEN BULKE	Former Volley-ball international, Doctor in Medicine and Anthropology, graduate of the Palo Alto Mental Research Institute, teacher, researcher, author, public speaker (AFACE), APM expert, Founding President of *Succeed Together®*, a firm which builds tools to assist in Enterprise management, based on three expert domains: teaching how to question, fast synthesis of verbal contributions and technical mastery of platforms for interaction and collaboration.	Member
David CHAVALARIAS	Graduate of *École Normale* (mathematics & informatics) agrégé in mathematics, Doctor in Cognitive Science (*École Polytechnique*), works as CNRS research director and as director of the *Complex Systems Institute Paris Ile-de-France* (http://iscpif.fr). Main research activities are on Computational social science, Modelling of cultural dynamics, Web text mining and Quantitative epistemology. https://iscpif.fr/chavalarias/	Member

Research Support Circle

Name	Brief career notes; Perspectives
Jean-Louis LE MOIGNE	Emeritus professor at *Aix-Marseille Université*, facilitator of *Réseau Intelligence de la Complexité* (www.mcxapc.org). Researches the epistemology of complexity, the modelling of complex systems and organisation engineering disciplines. https://en.wikipedia.org/wiki/Jean-Louis_Le_Moigne
François FLAHAULT	Emeritus Research director (CNRS) (EHSS) Philosopher, ethnologist. Practices transdisciplinary research in psychology, biology and general anthropology. Examines the Western concept of humans and society and the conditions of psychic existence of human beings. http://francoisflahault.fr/beliefs.php
Paul BOURGINE	President of the *Complex Systems Digital Campus* (CS-DC, an UNESCO UniTwin), Honorary president of RNSC (*Réseau National des Systèmes Complexes*), Former director of *CREA-Ecole Polytechnique* (Research Centre for Applied Epistemology). Paul Bourgine has always led the way on initiatives concerning the economy, cognitive science and complexity. https://www.researchgate.net/profile/Paul_Bourgine
Emmanuel SANDER	Director of Doctoral School *Cognition, Langage, Interaction*, associate director of *Laboratoire Paragraphe*. Also founding member of LabEx *H2H : Arts et médiations humaines*. Among other work, researches the role of analogy in cognition. https://www.researchgate.net/profile/Emmanuel_Sander

Name	Brief career notes; Perspectives
René DOURSAT	Research Scientist, http://doursat.free.fr/ Works on research at the interface between Artificial intelligence, complex systems and biology. Has created a new area of research on *meta-design*, exploring the morphogenesis of artificial systems drawing their inspiration from living things.
Henri CESBRON-LAVAU	Head of seminars at Sainte-Anne Hospital (Paris), Psychoanalyst in residence, AMA psychanalyst of the International Lacanian Association Head of the seminar in psychoanalysis at *École Polytechnique* and of a seminar on Psychic reality and Objective illusions, Co-founder of *Matinées lacaniennes*.
Mehdi KHAMASSI	CNRS researcher in Robotics and neuroscience (UPMC), HDR in biology Works on the relationships among mind, cognition, intelligent systems and robots.
Frédéric DECREMPS	Professor of Physics at UPMC, head of the dual training *Sciences et Design* (UPMC, in partnership with ENSCI-Les ateliers), co-facilitator of "Démarche scientifique et esprit critique".
Arnaud BANOS	During the last 10 years, he directed the Complex Systems Institute of Paris and the research lab Géographie-cités in Paris. He is currently a full time member of the research unit IDEES in Normandie, France and leads the Lab of Excellence DynamiTe in Paris. Access to his publications. https://www.cnrs-univ-arizona.net/biographies/arnaud-banos/

Acknowledgments

The author of this manifesto is Michel Paillet, president of "Welcome Complexity". As such, he is responsible for its content. This 'individual' could never have written this manifesto without the human chain (or rather the rhizome) of the authors who preceded and nourished it. The main influences, direct or indirect, are as follows: the currents of critical thinking in philosophy (Herbert Marcuse, Jurgen Habermas), the currents of thinking in complexity, systems thinking, constructivism, pragmatism and cognitive sciences (Jean Piaget, Herbert Simon, Francisco Varela, Edgar Morin, Jean-Louis Le Moigne, John Dewey), currents of thought on the interiority of the human being and the feeling of existing (Martin Buber, Carl Gustav Jung, Irvin Yalom, François Flahault), currents of anthropological thought on narrative (Vladimir Propp, Joseph Campbell).

A requirement of the manifesto was an explicit or tacit approval from a rooted and multi-disciplinary perspective. I would like to thank all people from the research circle support (refer to the appendices). All of them read the first drafts of the French version, provided suggestions and gave me an approval.

I would like to give a special mention to Jean-Louis Le Moigne, who has always been present for me each time I needed to discuss a specific semantic issue, and François Flahault. They have been thorough and careful readers of the full French version which would not be what it is without their support.

The French version also benefited from cross contributions from Philippe Fleurance, Dominique Genelot, Paul Bourgine, Emmanuel Sander, Henri Cesbron-Lavau, Mehdi Khamassi, René Doursat, Arnaud Banos, Frédéric Decremps, Laurent Daniel, Jérémie Averous, Jean-Pierre Dandrieux, Jérôme Lazard, Brice de Gromard, Emilie Coubat, Léa Abourousse.

I would like to especially thank our translator, Jean-Pierre Paillet (PhD linguistic), who did an impressive and remarkable translation work.

I would like then to thank our editor Anne-Claire Chêne (PhD), who went through all the text to challenge our translator and our publisher, Jérémie Averous, who gave the final shape and published the present work.

Index

P

S

U

W

www.ingramcontent.com/pod-product-compliance
Ingram Content Group UK Ltd.
Pitfield, Milton Keynes, MK11 3LW, UK
UKHW040002200726
13854UKWH00001B/1

9 789811 477720